LITERACY & AWARENESS

David Wray

Hodder & Stoughton

A MEMBER OF THE HODDER HEADLINE GROUP

In association with the United Kingdom Reading Association

For Jane

Cataloguing in Publication Data is available from the British Library

ISBN 0-340-53180-0

First published 1994
Impression number   10 9 8 7 6 5 4 3 2 1
Year   1998   1997   1996   1995   1994

Typeset by Rowland Phototypesetting Limited, Bury St Edmunds, Suffolk.
Printed in Great Britain for Hodder & Stoughton Educational, a division of
Hodder Headline Plc, 338 Euston Road, London NW1 3BH by
Page Bros (Norwich) Ltd.

Contents

Introduction

From its roots in theories about the learning of foreign languages, interest in the topic of language awareness has grown rapidly over the last decade and its relevance to the learning of first languages and of the processes and skills of literacy has been increasingly stressed. The pioneering work of Hawkins (1984), which first put forward a utilitarian view of the concept of language awareness, has found echo in research and other scholarship (James and Garrett, 1991), in official documents such as the Kingman report (D.E.S., 1988) and the Cox report (D.E.S., 1989) and in a plethora of recent publications aimed at teachers of English at all levels (Carter, 1990; Harris and Wilkinson, 1990; Bain, Fitzgerald and Taylor, 1992; Haynes, 1992). Language awareness, often referred to as Knowledge About Language (KAL) although the two terms are conceptually different, has become enshrined as part of the National Curriculum for English and become a focus of a great deal of pre- and in-service training energy.

The area has not been without its controversies, one of which has been the fate of the very expensive Language in the National Curriculum (LINC) project. While this particular problem occurred for political reasons, there have also been many theoretical and practical problems raised and debated in the course of research and development work on the concept of language awareness in its widest sense. These have included debates over the nature of language awareness itself. The impetus of the work of Hawkins (1984) led to a definition of this as 'a person's sensitivity to and conscious awareness of the nature of language and its role in human life' (Donmall, 1985, p. 7) and the teaching of it as a body of descriptive knowledge about the structures and functions of language with the assumption that this would in some way contribute to improvements in the use of language. This view, tacitly accepted by the Kingman committee (D.E.S., 1988), has been heavily criticised by those arguing from a more critical perspective, such as Ivanic (1990). Ivanic and her colleagues (Clark, Fairclough, Ivanic and Martin-Jones,

1990, 1991) argue that the study of language which does not make reference to the close relation between language structure and power relationships deprives students of the chance to understand how they might exercise greater control over the ways they use language and the ways in which language affects their lives.

Increasing interest in the concept of language awareness has been paralleled by a growth in research and study of the psychological concept of metacognition. Stemming from the work of Vygotsky (1962), who suggested that there are two stages in the development of knowledge (first, its automatic unconscious acquisition and, secondly, a gradual increase in active conscious control over that knowledge), there has been burgeoning interest in the distinction between cognitive and metacognitive aspects of knowledge. The term metacognition refers to the deliberate conscious control of one's own cognitive actions (Brown, 1980) and has been defined by Flavell (1976) as follows:

> Metacognition refers to one's knowledge concerning one's own cognitive processes and products or anything related to them . . . Metacognition refers, among other things, to the active monitoring and conscious regulation and orchestration of these processes in relation to the cognitive objects or data on which they bear, usually in the service of some concrete goal or objective. (p. 232)

Its operation, especially during the process of reading, has been the focus of an enormous amount of American research over the past decade (although, as yet, little has been done in a British context), and understanding about the nature and effects of metacognition on both reading and writing processes has been considerably enhanced.

Language awareness and metacognition come together very strongly when one considers the processes of literacy, and it is the purpose of this book to examine both these areas in relation to their implications for the teaching of literacy. 'Awareness of the nature of language' and conscious control over the cognitive activities involved in literacy are clearly topics which should inform the teacher of literacy and language. It has, however, previously been difficult to find written attempts to treat these areas together and, especially, which try to investigate the implications for teaching of such a diverse range of research and study. This book attempts to do both these things by, first, surveying as thoroughly as possible what has been suggested about these topics by research studies from several parts of the world and, secondly, presenting and discussing the practical teaching implications of this body of work, particularly for teachers of literacy in primary schools. It should be noted that this work is steadily becoming more important, both theoretically and practically. The current proposals for revisions to the National Curriculum for English, for example, show evidence of its influence as, for instance, in their drawing upon the research into phonological awareness which I discuss in Chapter 3.

The book begins with a discussion of the Knowledge about Language issue and outlines in some detail the dimensions which knowledge about language includes and which might be focused upon in teaching. Chapter 2 looks at what children know about the process of reading and, more particularly, upon the late John Downing's controversial cognitive clarity theory. It sets the tone for the book by presenting a case for an 'aware' approach to teaching the processes of literacy. Chapter 3 continues the examination of the importance of awareness in the beginning stages of reading by looking at three further aspects, each of which have, in their own ways, important implications for approaches to teaching reading: syntactic awareness, phonological awareness and the awareness of the particular forms of language associated with books. Chapter 4 examines what we know about children's perceptions of the writing process and includes a discussion about the prevalence of function and form in approaches to early literacy and writing in particular. Chapter 5 moves on to a detailed examination of research into the operation of metacognition in reading comprehension and some of the implications of this large body of research into comprehension monitoring are discussed. Chapter 6 analyses the research on the role of awareness in writing. The final chapter of the book looks at some particular teaching strategies and suggests that there are some positive steps which teachers of literacy can take towards ensuring an 'aware' approach.

1 *Knowing about language*

Developments in thinking

There have been several distinct phases, or fashions, in the teaching of the English language to English schoolchildren. In reaction to a heavily grammar-based approach, probably familiar to many of us from our own school experience, English teaching in the 1970s changed its name, at least in primary schools, to language development, and became much more concerned with the ways children used language than what they explicitly knew about it. Children's awareness about how language worked was assumed to be developed intuitively from an extended experience of using language. The important aspect of this awareness was claimed to be, not knowledge about the forms of language, but sensitivity towards the functions of language and its effects upon others. Awareness was, therefore, seen as 'closely parallel to the kind of sensitivity towards human feeling and relationships which every teacher of English hopes to develop in his pupils through his use of literature' (Halliday, 1971, p. 9). Explicit discussion of this sensitivity was not seen as at all necessary to its development.

> . . . the development of awareness does not entail the learning of a body of facts about language. It is a process by which pupils come to understand much more fully than before the nature of their own experience as users of language. The degree to which this understanding comes to be formulated explicitly in what they say and write about language depends upon their own capacities and the judgement of those who teach them.
> (Halliday, 1971, p. 9)

The next swing of the pendulum was signalled by the HMI document 'English from 5 to 16' (D.E.S., 1984). HMI argued that, as a discrete aim in language development, children should be taught:

> . . . about language, so that they achieve a working
> knowledge of its structure and of the variety of ways in
> which meaning is made, so that they have a vocabulary for
> discussing it, so that they can use it with greater awareness,
> and because it is interesting. (p. 3)

Notwithstanding the tautology in the third of these reasons for teaching about language (children should be taught awareness so that they might have greater awareness!), the document had a significant influence upon national developments, and occasioned a great deal of controversy. It is at pains to state that it is not advocating isolated exercise in grammatical rules and that knowledge about language is much wider than this, yet its list of objectives for knowledge about language at age 11 consists entirely of statements about grammar. (It also includes the incredible objective that 11 year olds should know 'the rules of spelling' (p. 8). The most experienced linguistics experts in the world would be pushed to pass this one!)

Subsequently, the Kingman report (D.E.S., 1988) extended the idea of knowledge about language and produced a model of language comprising four elements. These were:

1 the forms of the English language;
2 (i) communication;
  (ii) comprehension;
3 acquisition and development;
4 historical and geographical variation.

The report argued that 'Successful communication depends upon a recognition and accurate use of the rules and conventions. Command of these rules and conventions is more likely to increase the freedom of the individual than diminish it' (para. 1.11). It suggested that helping children learn the rules is a 'subtle process which requires the teacher to intervene constructively and at an appropriate time' (para. 2.28). This should happen 'mainly through an exploration of the language pupils use, rather than through exercises out of context . . . so that explicit statement consolidates the implicit awareness and effective learning occurs' (para. 2.30).

This insistence that knowledge about language needed to be taught, but was best approached through meaningful contexts rather than isolated exercises, was taken up by the later Cox report (D.E.S., 1989), and was emphasised in the National Curriculum for English (D.E.S., 1990).

Later official commentary aimed to dilute the strength of this argument, however, claiming that teachers, particularly of early years children, found little direct teaching guidance in the National Curriculum orders (N.C.C., 1992). It remains the case, however, that many questions have still been begged and, for many commentators, the case for an explicit focus upon knowledge about language has not yet been fully argued.

I will now go on to look in more detail at aspects of this argument, beginning with an examination of the rationale for teaching knowledge about language. I will also discuss what knowing about language might involve and what might be taught, before concluding with a brief look at strategies for teaching.

Why know about language?

The documentation leading up to the National Curriculum requirements for English (D.E.S., 1989) argues strongly for the place of teaching about language. The argument consists of two strands.

> Two justifications for teaching pupils explicitly about language are, first, the positive effect on aspects of their use of language and secondly, the general value of such knowledge as an important part of their understanding of their social and cultural environment, since language has vital functions in the life of the individual and of society. (para. 6.6)

The second of these arguments is the less controversial, but may still need some elaboration. It rests on the assumption that language is central to individual and cultural identity. In many ways, understanding who we are involves understanding how we use language (and how language uses us). Language closely relates to identity in a number of ways, for example, in geographical, gender, ethnic and social dimensions.

In the geographical dimension, it is well known that it is often possible to identify where someone comes from by the way they talk. Regional variations within English may be accounted for by dialect, in which the variation is in terms of the vocabulary and the grammatical structures used, or by accent, in which the variation is in pronunciation. Giles (1971) demonstrated that speakers are often capable of shifting their accents in quite subtle ways depending upon the social situation in which they find themselves. This suggests an awareness of, first, the need to change and, secondly, the way this is achieved. Similarly, most people are multi-dialectal (or at least bi-dialectal in that they will command a regional dialect and the standard dialect known as Standard English) in that they are able to make shifts in their patterns of speech depending upon social situation. Someone from Lancashire attending a job interview will probably not address the interviewer as 'pal', although that would be quite common in an informal conversation with other speakers of the same dialect. Again, this ability to switch dialects suggests that the speakers have the awareness of the need to change, that is of the influence of social context upon language, and of the mechanisms of making the change, that is, knowing how one dialect differs from another.

In terms of gender, the association in English of a particular way of speaking with a particular sex is not as strong as in, for instance, Japanese, where males and females have distinct styles of speech available to them. In terms of frequency of usage, however, English female speakers are more likely than males to use such terms as 'Oh dear' and 'lovely', and also to ask more questions, make more encouraging noises such as 'mm', but interrupt and argue less (Crystal, 1987). This fits the supportive, rather than proactive, role women have traditionally been allotted in English society. If these linguistic stereotypes are broken, most speakers tend to notice the fact and its implications, which suggests a level of awareness of both the rules and the forms.

The importance of language to ethnic identity will be obvious to anyone who has seen road signs in Wales written in English, but daubed with the Welsh language equivalent. Ethnic groups, especially minority groups, tend to seek for ways to distinguish themselves from other groups, and language is an obvious, highly-noticeable means of doing this. Many such groups have more than one language at their disposal, and switch between them according to the social situation in which they find themselves. As an example of this, consider some 8 year olds in a primary school in Cardiff. These children were of Pakistani origin and spoke Gujerati at home and with some of their friends. On occasions at home, and at Saturday school, they learnt and spoke Urdu. For religious reasons, they were also learning Arabic, although this was not used conversationally. At school, they used English in class and with some of their friends but, because they were attending a bilingual school, they were also learning, and spoke in class, Welsh. This range is surprising enough in itself, but even more remarkable is that these children did not appear to be suffering from any emotional traumas because of their linguistic situation, neither did there seem to be much interference of one language with another. They rarely mixed the languages they were using, largely because each had a quite tightly-defined social context in which it was acceptable or expected. This socially dependent differentiation is quite common and suggests the presence of a considerable amount of language awareness in the speakers.

The relationship between language and social identity is also fairly clear. English is not in the position of other languages in having two separate standard language forms, one for ordinary conversation and one for special uses, primarily in formal speech and writing. This is the situation in, for example, Greek with its 'high' Katharevousa and its 'low' Demotic varieties, and Swiss German with Hochdeutsch used for formal purposes and Schweitzerdeutsch used in informal speech. English does, however, have social class distinctions in language which are perhaps more entrenched than in most languages. Most people will have encountered the distinctions popularised by Nancy Mitford between 'U' and 'non-U' usage, according to which it is 'U' (or upper class) to have luncheon with vegetables followed by pudding, and 'non-U' to have dinner with greens followed by a sweet. Although terms and words continue to change with the current fashion, the denoting of certain language forms as 'not quite right for the situation' remains. In order to survive linguistically, without making fools of themselves, people who move between different social situations (which means most of us in these more socially mobile times) need to have the awareness to recognise the demands of particular contexts and to select the appropriate forms to use.

In each of these dimensions of language and identity, it has been pointed out that language users require a great deal of knowledge about language and its contexts in order to manoeuvre successfully within their linguistic repertoires. People unable to do this are trapped in inappropriate uses which can lead to quite serious social handicaps. Linguistic awareness allows control over the language system as it relates to social needs. The issue cannot be whether linguistic awareness is beneficial or not; this is beyond reasonable doubt. What is at issue, and extremely controversial, is how language users develop this awareness, and whether it can be explicitly taught, as the first argument advanced in the Cox report claims. Does explicit teaching have positive effects upon children's use of language?

This argument is controversial because it tends to be linked with calls for a return to the formal teaching of grammatical rules about which many teachers are justifiably suspicious (they doubt it will have an effect upon children's subsequent use of language). The Cox report admits that 'it is true that it has been difficult or impossible to show any direct cause-and-effect relation between teaching formal grammar and improved writing performance' (D.E.S., 1989, para. 6.8). This is, in fact, understating the position. It is reasonably well established from research findings that instruction in, and knowledge of, formal grammar bears no relationship to competence in language use, as the review by Wilkinson (1971) comprehensively demonstrated. Both Cox and Kingman, however, explicitly reject a return to formal grammar teaching, preferring instead a much broader approach. They recommend that knowledge about language work should cover the following material:

- *Language variation according to situation, purpose, language mode, regional or social group.* This would cover the usage and forms of dialects, accents and registers, as well as the influences of context upon language and the differences between speech and writing. Work of this nature would, it is argued, make children more tolerant of linguistic variety and more aware of the richness of language.

- *Language in literature.* This covers the use of language for particular stylistic effects, and the implication is that explicitly studying the way writers use language may enable children to incorporate a range of stylistic devices into their own writing, as well as increasing their responsiveness to literature.

- *Language variation across time.* This would cover the ways in which language usage, both grammatical constructions and vocabulary, change historically. Again the argument is that knowledge of this would make pupils more sensitive users of language.

Although the National Curriculum recommendation is for this material to be taught through meaningful contexts of language use, which seems to make more sense than attempting any isolated teaching, it has still to be admitted that the central point of the argument is not yet proven. The recommendation is based upon belief rather than evidence. It may, indeed, be the case that the proposition that there is a cause-and-effect relationship between particular kinds of teaching and linguistic skill is unprovable, given the impossibility of isolating particular linguistic experiences from one another. We have to look elsewhere for clear guidance on the place of teaching.

This same issue recurs in consideration of the relationship of linguistic awareness to all areas of literacy, as we shall see in the following chapters. Baldly stated, it concerns the question of whether linguistic awareness can be taught directly in such a way that it leads to improved linguistic performance, or whether increased awareness is itself a product of broadening experience of language use.

What does knowledge about language consist of?

Notwithstanding the rather 'chicken and egg' question of how it develops, it is still necessary to clarify what is involved in language awareness. What 'knowledge about language' would competent language users be expected to have?

Much of our understanding on this topic has come from the work of those concerned with the learning and teaching of second languages, particularly Hawkins (1984). Garvie (1990) gives a useful framework incorporating several types of language awareness. These types will be discussed separately under the headings she gives them.

Linguistic awareness

This refers to a knowledge of the basic components of language, that is, the letters, morphemes and words which can be arranged in varying ways to signify meaning. It also includes the knowledge that these components are manoeuvrable.

When asked questions such as, 'What letter does the word "unicorn" begin with?', competent language users will be able to specify the correct one, even though the sound made at the beginning of this word can also be represented by 'y'. Similarly, when presented with a selection of words such as, 'forswink', 'zbastit', 'mpopo' and 'glenkin', English language users will have little trouble in distinguishing those which might possibly be English words, even if they have never actually met them before, from those which could not be English.

Language users also have a fair degree of morphemic awareness, that is, an awareness of the smallest elements of meaning contained in words. (As an example, the word 'exported' has three morphemes: 'port', indicating the kind of action implied, 'ex', indicating the direction of this action, and 'ed', indicating the tense of the verb.) They will have little trouble with puzzles such as the following:

This is a blonk. If another blonk comes, there will be
two _____.
Today I must ruggle my bedroom. I should have _____ it
yesterday.

It would be interesting to assess the level of awareness of these things held
by young children. Research by Berko (1958) suggested that quite young
children were able to complete successfully morpheme puzzles similar to
those given above. Yet other research by, for example, Reid (1966), has
demonstrated that young children often seem confused between terms such
as 'letter', 'word', etc. Research such as this will be discussed in more detail
in Chapter 2, but two points should be noted here. The first is that it is
extraordinarily difficult to actually find out what young children know
about language. Most researchers resort to versions of simply asking them,
but never really know whether children who cannot reply do not know
the relevant facts about language or merely cannot express their
knowledge.

The second point relates to this and concerns the importance of having
a language with which to talk about language. Terms such as 'word',
'letter', etc. are part of a metalanguage which may be an important part
of linguistic awareness, but is certainly not all there is to it. Many
discussions of teaching in this area seem to confuse knowledge about
language with knowledge of this metalanguage. We shall return to this
point later in this chapter.

Psycholinguistic awareness

The competent language user not only knows about the components of
language, but also the rules for fitting these together. Language is a
thoroughly ordered system, or interacting set of systems. There are three
major systems.

The phonological system

According to this:

1 Certain sounds are more likely to follow others. English speakers
   do not expect, and find it difficult to pronounce, words which begin
   with the letter combinations 'mb' and 'zd', yet these would be
   normal combinations to Zulu and Russian speakers respectively.

2 Some sounds can be run into one another or missed out entirely.
   Speakers know that it is permissible to omit the 'o' sound in

'did not', but not in 'Didcot'; and to reduce 'and' to the sound 'n' in 'fish and chips', but not in 'left-hand side'.

3   Certain combinations of sounds can be stressed in different ways, which makes a difference to their meanings. Language users learn to tell the difference between 'suspéct' and 'súspect' and between 'convíct' and 'cónvict'.

The lexical system

According to this, words are tailored to play their correct roles in sentences. This involves morphemic change and requires in the language user an extension of the morphemic awareness referred to earlier. Not only can he or she correctly supply the word in 'Here is a blonk. Here is another blonk. Now there are two ＿＿', but he or she can also carry this awareness forward: 'Yesterday I saw a blonk who was carrying its satchel over its shoulder. Tomorrow I ＿＿ ＿＿ two ＿＿ who ＿＿ ＿＿ carrying ＿＿ ＿＿ over ＿＿ ＿＿.'

The syntactic system

This determines appropriate word orders and allows speakers of English to reject combinations such as, 'I not can carry this bag heavy' which, literally translated, would be acceptable in French. So powerful is language users' awareness of appropriate order that it can constrain them to reorder incorrect sequences. Kolers (1973) found that adult readers would often read sentences such as the following, which had been literally translated from the French, 'His horse made resound the earth', with the correct English order, remaining quite unconscious of the fact.

Kolers also found that when readers made mistakes with words they were extremely likely to retain the word's syntactic function, reading nouns for nouns, verbs for verbs, etc., thus suggesting a high level of syntactic awareness. This kind of awareness has also been found in 6 year olds by Weber (1970) and in 5 year olds by Clay (1972). In both cases, it was found that when these young readers made mistakes in reading words, the words they substituted would most often be the same part of speech as the original. Syntactic awareness seems to develop fairly early in language careers.

Discourse awareness

The language user also needs to be aware of the rules for the combination of the elements of language at a level higher than the sentence. This means knowing how meaning is carried forward from one sentence to the next, either through connective words such as 'and', 'therefore' and 'however', or through the inter-sentence referencing system which Halliday and Hasan (1976) refer to as 'cohesive ties'.

Crystal (1976) claims that children are able to use simple connectives from about the age of 3 years, and can often sustain quite long discourses this way: 'Daddy gone in the garden – and he felled over – and he hurt his knee – and Mummy gave him a plaster – and he didn't cry.' They may use other connectives, such as 'but', ''cos', etc., but it is not until quite a while later (around 7 according to Crystal) that they begin to use more complex adverbial connectors, such as 'actually', 'although' and 'really'.

Cohesion is the device used in language to refer ideas from one part of a discourse to another. In order to sustain understanding over a long discourse, the language user relies upon an awareness of how cohesion operates. 'Cohesion arises at any point in a text where the meaning of some aspect of text can only be determined by reference to information contained somewhere else in the text' (Wallach and Miller, 1988, p. 122). The term 'text' here can refer to either written or spoken discourse. There are several ways in which this works:

1. *Reference*: semantic relations achieved through use of words, usually pronouns, to refer to objects or ideas mentioned elsewhere in a text:
   John lifted his bag. *It* seemed very heavy.

2. *Lexical*: relations achieved through vocabulary selection, usually by synonyms or word repetition:
   I like cats. They are such lovable *animals*.
   We live in a house. It's a really nice *house*.

3. *Conjunction*: relations achieved through the use of connectors to show the relationships between statements:
   She was smiling, *but* she did not seem happy.
   When you have finished, we shall leave.

4. *Substitution*: relations achieved by using one word or phrase in place of another:
   I bought a new car today. There were *several* I could have had.

5. *Ellipsis*: relations established by deleting words or phrases:
   Who brought the parcel? The postman (*brought it*).

Little is known about the development of children's abilities to handle these language forms in speech, although Stoel-Gammon and Hedberg (1984) suggest that referential and lexical cohesion appear first in children's language, followed by conjunction, substitution and ellipsis. Little sophistication in the use of cohesive devices is found before the age of 8 or so. The work of Chapman (1983) confirms this rather late development by concentrating upon the use of cohesion in reading. He found that while an understanding of the use of cohesive ties (the use of pronoun references in this case) was associated with ability in reading, there were still many children aged 13 or 14 who found difficulty with this. Discourse awareness seems relatively late to develop, yet the texts which children in junior and early secondary schools are expected to handle are complex in their use of discourse linking devices.

Communicative awareness

The language user also needs to be aware of the ways in which words, strings of words and full discourse can change depending upon such influences as topic, purpose, situation and audience. Language is usually more than a string of words selected to represent a sequence of meanings for its producer. It is normally intended to have an effect upon another person, that is, to communicate. There are many ways of expressing the same thing, and the way which is chosen is usually that appropriate to the particular situation. Most language users will be aware, for example, of the difference between, 'I do hope you don't mind me mentioning it but I'm afraid you're standing on my toe', and 'Get off my toe, you clumsy lump!', and would respond in an appropriate way. Linguists refer to this dimension of language use and awareness as 'pragmatics' (Naremore and Hopper, 1990) and skill in its use has been termed 'communicative competence' by Hymes (1972).

> We have then to account for the fact that a normal child
> acquires knowledge of sentences, not only as grammatical, but
> also as appropriate. He or she acquires competence as to
> when to speak, when not, and as to what to talk about
> with whom, when, where, in what manner. In short, a child
> becomes able to accomplish a repertoire of speech acts,
> to take part in speech events, and to evaluate their
> accomplishment by others.
> (Hymes, 1972, p. 277)

Young children exposed to a variety of language situations naturally learn to make adjustments to their language production. They will speak in a different way to their friends in the playground than they do to their teacher in the classroom, and in a still different way to their teddy bear or doll. Communicative awareness seems to develop relatively early, simply through experience.

Sociolinguistic awareness

This form of awareness links very closely with that just described, and implies an understanding of the influence of social context upon the language used. It extends communicative awareness to include a sensitivity to factors such as status and role, which influence the degree of formality in communication and to the factors which determine when a particular style of language usage should be switched to another, more appropriate one. I discussed earlier the fact that most competent language users have a variety of dialects and accent forms at their disposal, and make reasonably sensitive judgements about which a particular social situation requires.

Most adults do this all the time, simply because not to do so would lead to them being looked down on by other people. The motivation of social approval is usually a powerful one. Some examples of this would include the development of specialised vocabulary and language structures among teenage sub-cultures, and the exclusiveness of the talk among interest groups, such as computer clubs. To become full members of any of these groups, one has to demonstrate an ability to use an appropriate style of language.

Language variations dependent upon social contexts are usually known as registers. The contexts in which registers are used also vary, chiefly in their degree of formality. When we visit our solicitor, for example, we are likely to use a different register of language than when we are relaxing with our friends. The language we use in these situations will vary in several ways:

- *Vocabulary*: we are more likely to use slang expressions, or word-approximations, such as 'thingummy', in informal contexts.

- *Syntax*: in formal situations we are more likely to use Standard English forms, whereas in informal situations we will probably use such forms as contractions ('can't', 'innit'), incomplete sentences, and dialect structures.

- *Pace*: in informal situations we tend to speak fairly quickly, whereas in formal contexts we generally use a more measured pace.

- It would clearly be as incorrect to use a formal way of speaking in an informal situation as the other way round. The 'correct' way of speaking is that which is appropriate to the situation.

The matching of register to situation is something most of us do without really thinking about it. We simply use language in the way which 'feels right'. This ability to sense appropriateness is clearly, however, learned from experience, and we would expect speakers with more limited experience to be less skilled at it. Just how early in children's linguistic careers this begins to happen is suggested by a fascinating study reported by Andersen (1990). She recorded the language used by 4 to 7 year olds as they engaged, using puppets, in dramatic play set either in home, doctor's surgery or school classroom settings. Although there was some difference in skill at register switching between these groups, all these children showed an awareness of the need and the means to alter their choice of vocabulary, syntax, topic and speech pitch to fit the roles they were playing. They showed an awareness of status differences between, for example, doctors and nurses, teachers and children and, significantly, fathers and mothers. These distinctions were made whatever their personal experience of these situations had been like. For example, fathers were always portrayed as 'in business' and in control, with authoritative voices using many imperatives, and mothers as submissive and home-bound, tending to ask rather than tell, even if the children's own parents were not at all like this. The study suggests that young children pick up register patterns from the language they hear all around them, not just in their homes, and quickly become skilled at making sociolinguistic distinctions.

Strategic awareness

The language user is also aware of a range of strategies which can be adopted when there are problems in communication. If, for example, the person to whom he or she is speaking evidently does not understand what is being said, the speaker will often try alternative tactics, such as speaking slower or using signs. If the speaker him or herself forgets particular words or phrases, he or she will adopt strategies to extricate him or herself from the problem, such as circumlocutions or appeals to the listener's ability to infer. The ability to do these things rests upon two aspects of awareness: first, a recognition that there is a problem and, secondly, knowledge of a range of strategies for dealing with it. Strategic awareness is important in the exercise of focused language skills, such as reading for understanding, as will be discussed in Chapter 5.

Young children also seem to develop this awareness comparatively early. Garvie (1990) gives the example of a 6-year-old second language learner who, when shown a picture of a mouse and asked what it was, substituted the unknown word with a scurrying movement of her fingers and the statement 'He do like dees'. It is probably the case that children only develop this form of language awareness through experience, since they are unlikely to be taught how to deal with language problems of this nature which they might have.

Teaching knowledge about language

As was stated earlier, the argument about whether direct teaching about language has any effect upon children's language awareness has not been proven. In the discussion so far about dimensions to language awareness, the point has been made several times that young children seem to develop knowledge in most of these areas simply through being users of language. This is not, however, a conclusive argument for not doing any direct teaching. It is still possible to argue that by bringing language awareness to the foreground in children's minds, teaching might make knowledge more explicit and thereby increase conscious control over language. This is in essence the argument used in the Kingman report (D.E.S., 1988) when it put forward that 'there is no positive advantage in . . . ignorance [about the structure and uses of language]' (paragraph 1.12).

Many of the concepts outlined above could be explicitly focused upon in classroom teaching, and there is no intrinsic reason why children should not find the study of their own language as fascinating as they might find any other topic covered in school. Programmes such as those described by Hudson (1985), Redfern (1985) and Robins (1985) would be recognised as worthwhile by most teachers of primary and middle school children.

In the course of programmes such as these, an extra dimension would almost inevitably be involved. This is the use of language to discuss language. In discussing dialects, for example, children would have to use words to describe differences and particular features. They would thus need to use a metalanguage. This might well include terms associated traditionally with formal grammar teaching, such as phrase, sentence, verb and adjective, but would need to be wider than this since it would deal with language functions as well as forms. It would need, for example, to have ways of describing the difference between, 'I'm very sorry to disturb you, but I wonder if you would mind just moving your suitcase a little?', and 'I do wish you would move this. It's really in my way.' The need for this metalanguage is highlighted by the inclusion in the National Curriculum (D.E.S., 1990) of attainment targets such as the following (all at Level 5) which I have paraphrased:

Pupils should be able to:

- talk about variations in vocabulary between different regional or social groups;

- talk about variations in vocabulary according to purpose, topic and audience and according to whether language is spoken or written;

- recognise and talk about the use of word play and some of the effects of the writer's choice of words in imaginative uses of English.

Although it is essential to recognise that such a metalanguage is the means to, rather than the aim of, language awareness work, it is necessary to raise the question of whether those responsible for the teaching of such work themselves have sufficient command of it to be helpful. From the limited research which has been done in this area (Wray, 1993), it appears that student teachers may not generally have an extensive knowledge of the requisite linguistic vocabulary.

Conclusion

It is possible to state some general principles which should underlie a direct study of language in primary schools. These follow from the knowledge we have about the role of language in making people what they are, and the fact that, by the time they reach school, the vast majority of children have already acquired more linguistic expertise than they have left to learn. Three principles can be stated:

First, schools and teachers should be aware of the expertise in language which their children bring to school with them, both in terms of a range of forms and in their awareness of the range of linguistic functions. This involves listening to the children and discussing things with them, but it may also involve more sustained attempts to forge links with local communities and with parents. In much work on language, it should be accepted that there will often be children in the class who are more expert in certain areas than the teacher.

Secondly, schools need to begin to work with their children as they are, rather than as they would like them to be. This means accepting that children bring a great deal of linguistic expertise to school with them and planning programmes to make the most of this, rather than to remediate perceived weaknesses. It also means attempting to create school and classroom environments in which children can feel confident that their language will be respected and is an appropriate vehicle for learning. As shown above, the task which children accomplish by themselves of not only learning the forms of a language, but also its pragmatic conventions and variations, is a substantial one. It will often be the case, however, that they have learned things about language upon which the school traditionally places little value. Schools need to revise their value systems if this is the case. All language knowledge is valuable.

Thirdly, schools should set themselves the goal of increasing the total language awareness of all their children. This means making language itself a much more prominent feature of classroom work. If children learn from experience, then the wider this experience can be, the wider the learning opportunities which ensue. No explicit teaching can take the place of meaningful experience. It might, however, enhance it.

If these principles lead to schools positively celebrating the language diversity within them, rather than either ignoring it or seeing it as a problem, it is likely that a great many social benefits will ensue as children begin to feel that their contributions to school life are important and valued. Whatever the educational arguments for and against the teaching of knowledge about language, these social arguments should not be overlooked. As pointed out earlier, language is more than a transparent channel of communication: it carries its own hidden curriculum which affects self-image and social relationships in profound ways about which teachers need to develop their own awareness.

2 *Awareness and the development of reading: confusion or clarity?*

Introduction

As with knowledge about language generally, there has been considerable debate about the role of awareness in the development of the ability to read. This debate has involved the question of whether awareness precedes, and is a cause of, successfully learning to read, or whether it is itself a product of this learning. Some aspects of this question will be examined in the following chapter. Here, however, I shall discuss another long-running aspect of this debate, that is, whether it is a characteristic feature of young children that they are unclear of the purposes for, and mechanisms of, reading.

Theorists and researchers working from a psychological tradition have found children to be very unclear about what reading is for and what it involves. A unifying theory, known as the 'cognitive clarity theory', has been put forward to explain these findings, and in the first part of this chapter I shall discuss this theory and its background, beginning with its characterisation of reading as a skilled behaviour. Later, I shall discuss some objections to this theory and its consequent diagnosis of young children as readers, using largely the insights which have been derived from the relatively new perspective of emergent literacy. Finally, in attempting to bring together the two sides of this debate, I shall put forward what seem to be the chief implications for teaching.

Reading as a skilled behaviour

Analysts of reading often refer to the 'reading process' to describe what they attempt to analyse. This term, however, has been criticised as a vague term which has no technical meaning in psychology, and is of little help in considering how reading is learnt (McNaughton, 1987). Clay's (1972) definition of reading clarifies the situation a little.

> Reading is a process by which a child can, on the run, extract
> a sequence of cues from the printed text and relate these,
> one to another, so that he understands the precise message
> of the text. The child continues to gain in this skill
> throughout his entire education, interpreting statements of
> ever-increasing complexity. (p. 8)

This use of the term 'skill' to describe the ability to perform the actions, mental and physical, which make up reading has had support from several other psychological investigators (e.g. McNaughton, 1987). McDonald's (1965) definition of a skill is useful here:

> From a psychological point of view, playing football or chess,
> or using a typewriter or the English language correctly demands
> complex sets of responses – some of them cognitive, some
> attitudinal and some manipulative. It is emphasised that
> this is not simply a matter of motor behaviour and that the
> player needs to understand the game, enjoy it and have
> the right attitudes about winning and losing. The total
> performance . . . is a complex set of processes – cognitive,
> attitudinal and manipulative. This complex integration of
> processes is what we usually mean when we refer to a
> skill. (p. 387)

Reading seems to fit this description as it involves complex relationships between cognitive, attitudinal and manipulative behaviours. Especially important for the purposes of this book is the inclusion of, in the components of skilled behaviour, the need for an understanding of what the activity is for and what it consists of.

In terms of the learning of skills it has been suggested (Fitts and Posner, 1967; Cronbach, 1977) that there are three phases in development. These are termed the cognitive, mastery and automaticity phases. In the cognitive phase, the learner must find out what is involved in the skill by 'getting in mind just what is to be done' (Cronbach, 1977, p. 398). So the task must be correctly understood right at the start. In the mastering phase, learners work at perfecting performance and practise accuracy. When this has been mastered, the skill is practised beyond mastery into the automaticity phase. This allows the process to become automatic so that it can be performed without effort when required, unless an unusual problem arises.

It is important to realise that, in the case of an extremely complex skill such as reading, these phases will occur and recur many times as different facets of the skill may develop at different rates. As this is a continuous process, it can be seen that the cognitive aspect of skill acquisition is vital in reading, especially in the early stages when so many aspects of the skill are new. Children who fail to understand the full purpose and nature of their early reading instruction may then remain trapped in the cognitive phase, trying hard to perform effectively at what they think the task involves, but being held back by this faulty conceptualisation. This would be likely to affect their attitudes to reading and hook them into a vicious cycle of:

- not understanding what they should be trying to achieve;

- therefore not achieving any easy command of the activity;

- therefore rejecting the activity and avoiding its practice;

- therefore failing to develop any deeper understanding of its purpose and nature.

The cognitive clarity theory of learning to read

In her review of research on the causes of reading disability, Vernon (1957) concluded that 'the fundamental and basic characteristic of reading disability appears to be cognitive confusion' (p. 71). In a later extension to the review, she developed this concept further:

> It would seem that in learning to read it is essential for the child to realise and understand the fundamental generalisation that in alphabetic writing all words are represented by combinations of a limited number of visual symbols . . . But a thorough grasp of this principle necessitates a fairly advanced stage of conceptual reasoning, since this type of organisation differs fundamentally from any previously encountered by children in their normal environment. (Vernon, 1971, p. 85)

Examples of this kind of confusion have been given by Clay (1972), including the case of one little boy who complained in tears that he could not read a page because of 'all those little white rivers' (p. 37). It should be noted, however, that the kind of confusion referred to by

Vernon is limited to that brought about by a failure to understand the ways in which print operates. Some theorists suggest that children's confusions about reading can be wider than this, and can extend to a bewilderment about the purpose of the whole enterprise.

Following Vernon's work, Downing (1979) advanced a theory about the need for cognitive clarity in successful readers:

> Cognitive confusion is the chief symptom of reading disability, according to Vernon. Therefore, if we generalise from her finding, we may postulate that cognitive clarity should be the typical characteristic of the successful reader. (p. 10)

Thus task awareness was seen to be a vital component in the acquisition of the skill of reading. In his development of the cognitive clarity theory, Downing (1979) begins from the argument of Mattingly (1972) that reading is a secondary activity dependent upon the reader's awareness of the workings of the primary linguistic activities of speaking and listening. This is in direct contradiction to the assertion of psycholinguistic theorists such as Smith (1971) and Goodman (1976) that reading and listening are parallel processes and both proceed without conscious awareness of how they work. Goodman advances the argument (Goodman and Goodman, 1977) that the learning of oral and written language are both normal consequences of being brought up in an environment founded upon people talking, reading and writing, and neither requires the learner to be 'aware' of their technical workings. In a similar way, learning to drive a car, another complex skill, does not demand of the learner an understanding of the working of the internal combustion engine. The learner does, however, require an understanding of what driving is and what it is for. Goodman, likewise, admits that an awareness of the purposes and uses of language is required in order to learn to read.

It should be noted that there has been considerable debate about whether learning to use spoken and written language are parallel or sequential achievements (see Hynds, 1990; Bald, 1990). Distinguished writers such as Donaldson (1989) and Perera (1984) have argued that literacy is learnt in quite different ways to speech and, of necessity, builds upon spoken language learning. Their arguments, however, rest upon a classification of spoken language learning as 'natural', which is itself a rather romantic idea. Children brought up in a non-speaking environment do not learn to speak, which suggests that speaking requires teaching.

The distinction in types of awareness is carried forward by Downing (1984) in his suggestion that linguistic awareness depends upon certain linguistic concepts. He identifies these as functional concepts and featural concepts. Functional concepts are ideas about the communication purpose of language, the purpose and function of reading. Featural concepts are about the representation of spoken language as symbols and include ideas about graphophonic information. He incorporates both these sets of concepts into his cognitive clarity theory (Downing, 1979), the revised statement of which incorporates eight postulates (Downing, 1986):

1 Writing or print in any language is a visible code for those aspects of speech that were accessible to the linguistic awareness of the creators of that code or writing system.

2 This linguistic awareness of the creators of a writing system included simultaneous awareness of the communicative function of language and certain features of spoken language that are accessible to the speaker–hearer for logical analysis.

3 The learning to read process consists in the rediscovery of (a) the functions and (b) the coding rules of the writing system.

4 Their rediscovery depends on the learner's linguistic awareness of the same features of communication and language as were accessible to the creators of the writing system.

5 Children approach the tasks of reading instruction with only partially developed concepts of the function and features of speech and writing.

6 Under reasonably good conditions, children develop increasing cognitive clarity about the functions and features of language.

7 Although the initial stage of literacy acquisition is the most vital one, conceptual challenges continue to arise and thus broaden the range of clarity throughout the later stages of education as new sub-skills are added to the student's repertory.

8 The cognitive clarity theory applies to all languages and writing systems.

Downing (1986) cites a great deal of cross-cultural research to suggest that language awareness, as defined by his theory, is a necessary element in early success in reading. Theorists arguing from a psycholinguistic and a socio-cultural perspective would not disagree with him with regard to the necessity for young children to have appropriate functional and featural concepts about reading. Children have to understand what they are trying to achieve. There is disagreement, however, about the extent of understanding about the functions of reading which children do have when they come to school. Harste, Woodward and Burke (1984) state very confidently: 'After many years of work in this area, however, we have yet to find a child who is "cognitively confused"' (p. 15). We need to examine the evidence on both sides of this question before a resolution can be attempted.

Children's concepts about reading

A great deal of research has enquired into children's thoughts about what the act of reading involved, most of them actually asking children at some point, 'What is reading?'. Some of these studies will be reviewed in this section (see Johns, 1986, for a more detailed review).

The earliest studies of concepts about reading seem to have concerned children with reading problems. Edwards (1958) interviewed 66 disabled readers of between 8 and 10 years of age and asked them what they and their parents thought was good reading when they started school. A large number described good reading as involving speed and fluency. Glass (1968) also found an emphasis on speed of reading in his interviews with poor readers of all school ages. Edwards suggested that many children were not aware that getting meaning was the purpose of reading, and that this lack of knowledge could produce retardation that resulted in inefficient reading strategies. Johns (1970) reached similar conclusions when he found that 1 out of 12 severely disabled readers answered 'I don't know' to the question 'What is reading?'. He suggested that these readers had been handicapped by their failure to understand what was involved in reading.

Several studies have concentrated on very young children, and that by McConkie (1959) has been the prototype for many studies. McConkie interviewed 81 5-year-old children and asked them the question, 'What do you think reading is?' Responses ranged from 'reading is telling stories' to 'reading is when you look at books then go home'. Only 11 per cent could express the idea that reading was a means of getting information, and only about one-quarter indicated that reading had anything to do with words or letters.

Mason (1967) asked 178 pre-schoolers a series of questions to study their concepts of reading. One question was 'Do you like to read?' By the time half the children had been interviewed, the investigators realised that most of the children had said they could read. The interviewers then asked the remaining 80 children 'Can you read all by yourself?' Over 90 per cent said they could. Mason's conclusion was that 'one of the first steps in learning to read is learning that one does not already know how' (Mason, 1967, p. 132). To many infant teachers who value a positive self-concept in creating confident learners, this conclusion would be questionable. An alternative might be that a first step in learning to read is gaining a fuller picture of what the process involves.

One of the most often cited studies was conducted by Reid (1966). This involved 12 5-year-olds, randomly selected from an Edinburgh class, who were interviewed three times in their first school year using a loose interview format which had a core of questions which could be asked in any order depending how the interview progressed. Reid noted that, although most of the children were aware that they could not read, very few had precise notions about reading and some were even unclear what marks on the page they were reading. Reid suggests that a constant effort to develop awareness of what reading is might facilitate early progress. There are, however, difficulties associated with this study. The most significant is recognised by Reid in a footnote:

> It may be argued, of course, that the fact that a child does not, when given opportunities to do so, use a certain term is not proof that it is unknown to him. This is true. He may, for instance, understand it when someone else uses it.
> (Reid, 1966, p. 58)

This problem resurfaces in later criticism of this type of study of reading concepts, as will be discussed later.

In order to consider to what extent these findings were determined by the interview method used, a study to replicate and expand Reid's work was undertaken by Downing (1970). Six boys and seven girls in their first school year in Hertfordshire were selected. The study used the loosely structured interviews employed by Reid, but also an experimental methodology and concrete stimuli. These three research methods produced findings that complement those of Reid, showing that pupils had only vague perceptions of the purposes and mechanics of reading.

Downing (1970) also questions whether teachers were making unwarranted assumptions about the children's perceptions of the nature of reading.

Denny and Weintraub (1966) report an investigation into the perceptions of reading held by 111 first-grade children (English Year 2) from widely divergent socio-economic backgrounds. The children were interviewed individually and asked three questions about reading:

1   Do you want to learn how to read?

2   Why?

3   What must you do to learn to read in first grade?

Analysis of the responses revealed that a quarter of these children could express no meaningful purpose for learning to read and a third had no idea how it was to be accomplished. In an early report of this research (Denny and Weintraub, 1963), 108 first graders' responses to the question, 'What is reading?' were analysed. Twenty-seven per cent of the responses were vague 'I don't know' answers. Object-related answers such as, 'when you read a book' constituted 33 per cent of responses, and 20 per cent of answers were cognitive, 'it helps you learn'. Denny and Weintraub (1966) stress the wide variety of early reading perceptions, including the 27 per cent of first-year children who could not verbalise their perception of the reading process.

In Johns and Johns (1971), 168 children of various ages were asked, among other questions, 'What is reading?' Seventy per cent of them gave vague, irrelevant or no responses, and only 4 per cent defined the process as involving both decoding and understanding. Johns (1986) reviews the results of several studies using this same question, and finds that most children either cannot respond intelligently to the question or characterise reading as to do with classroom procedures ('it's when you read to teacher') or objects ('it's reading from my reading book'). Few early readers seemed to associate reading with getting meaning.

The picture which seems to emerge from these studies is that the purpose of reading as a meaning-getting process is not really appreciated by many children, even as old as 12 and 13, although the older children do tend to appreciate this more than the younger (Johns and Ellis, 1976). Many children focus upon its decoding aspect (Tovey, 1976), although there is a great deal of vagueness about the precise mechanics of the process.

Still more children are unable to separate it from its place as a classroom procedure.

A problem with most of the studies reported so far, however, is their reliance upon the interview as the chief means of gathering information. It is at least possible that children may have understandings about the nature of reading and yet not be able to express these clearly. Indeed, many adults would have problems answering the question, 'What is reading?' Such abstract concepts are notoriously difficult to define, and the fact that you cannot answer such questions about them is no guarantee that you do not have an implicit understanding of them.

Support for this objection, and a totally different perspective upon children's concepts of reading, has come from the work of Goodman in the USA. She points out that abstract definitions are much harder to produce than contextually embedded understanding:

> Children can use language appropriately in context but when asked to define the same item, they often cannot. For example, part of the task we have given our readers is book handling. I hold up a page in a book, wave it back and forth and say, 'What is this?' None of the twelve 3 and 4 year olds I last did this with could answer the question. However, as I read them a story and came to the end of the print on the page, I'd say, 'What should I do now?' Everyone of the children I asked replied, 'Turn the page'. (Goodman, 1983, p. 73)

From a wide variety of research studies, Goodman produces evidence of the contextually embedded nature of children's understanding of reading. For example, she found (Goodman, 1986) that 60 per cent of the 3 year olds she studied, and 80 per cent of the 4 and 5 year olds, could read environmental print when it was embedded in its context. Thus they could read such things as the logos on toothpaste tubes, hamburger restaurant signs, etc. Any decontextualisation of these logos by, say, presenting them without their appropriate colour or surrounding designs, produced less accurate responses. Other researchers, such as Donaldson (1978), have also pointed out the importance of ensuring that children are in a meaningful context if we are to assess their understandings and abilities accurately. This suggests caution in interpreting the results of interview-based studies.

One of Goodman's findings which has great relevance in a discussion of children's understanding of the functions of reading is that the young children in her studies either provided accurate readings of environmental print items, or responded in terms of the item's function. A logo for a particular brand of milk might be read, for example, as 'milk', or 'it's good for you' (Goodman, 1986). This suggests not only a familiarity with environmental print, but also an understanding of the functions of print and print-labelled items. Goodman (1983) suggests that this demonstrates that awareness of function precedes that of form, and is, in fact, quite early to develop. Harste, Woodward and Burke (1984) come to a similar conclusion, and discuss the

> . . . expectation that written language is meaningful (i.e. has the function of telling us things). We do not know how or when children come to this important conclusion. All we know is that children as young as 3 have already made it, and that somehow readers who end up in remedial classes have lost it or lost faith in it. (p. 8)

This understanding of the functions of reading comes about, according to Hall (1987), in the same way as an understanding of the functions of spoken language, that is, through extended experience of a social context in which language is used for a particular function by significant others in that context. The social context determines the way language and literacy acts are perceived by children, and there have been several reported studies of children's socialisation into literate behaviour (Heath, 1983; Delgado-Gaitan, 1990). Common to these studies has been the finding that children in the communities studied, not those traditionally associated with educational success, are socialised into the uses of literacy relevant to their communities, not those valued by schools. This suggests that we should, as Street (1984) urges, talk about literacies as pluralistic rather than treat literacy as a monolithic concept.

Conclusion: towards a synthesis

On the face of it, the two strands of research which have been summarised in the previous sections are in complete contradiction with one another. On the one hand, young children are found to have a very limited conception of the purposes and ingredients of successful reading performance, yet on the other they are observed to behave in literate-like ways when faced with the meaningful print that surrounds them. How can this conflicting evidence be resolved?

One way of doing this, which Hall (1987) carries out comprehensively, is to explore the methodological and conceptual reasons why cognitive clarity researchers have failed to find in children the rich levels of awareness about the forms and functions of reading found by others working from an emergent literacy perspective. There is certainly scope for criticism of methods of investigation which rely heavily upon decontextualised interviews incorporating such abstract questions as 'What is reading?' It is also true that such investigations have almost without exception been framed as attempts to find out what children did not know about reading, rather than giving them opportunities to demonstrate what they did know.

A further point, which may be even more significant, is that investigations which have deliberately set out to examine children's concepts about reading have usually focused upon older children than those commonly reported upon in emergent literacy literature. Children of 5 and 6 years old are children with some experience of schooling and, particularly in the USA where kindergartens have tended to be organised along more formal lines than British nurseries, this schooling will probably have included some deliberate attempts to teach these children to read. It may be that it is actually this teaching which leads to children's confusion when asked questions about reading.

If this is a possibility, it is important to analyse what it may be about early school experience which brings about this confusion. This analysis is made by Ferreiro and Teberovsky (1983) in the conclusion to their study of pre-school children's awareness of reading and writing. It is worth quoting from this conclusion at some length.

> To understand print, preschool children have reasoned intelligently, elaborated good hypotheses about writing systems (although they may not be good in terms of our conventional writing system), overcome conflicts, searched for regularities, and continually attached meaning to written texts. But the logical coherence they impose upon themselves disappears when faced with what the teacher demands from them. They must worry about perception and motor control instead of the need to understand. They must acquire a series of skills instead of coming to know an object.

> They must set aside their own linguistic knowledge and capacity for thought until they discover, at a later period, that it is impossible to comprehend a written text without them. (p. 279)

What is being rejected here is the very notion of learning to read as the acquisition of a series of skills which lies at the heart of Downing's cognitive clarity theory. In its place is put the concept of learning to read as an act of knowledge construction, with the learner inventing and reinventing continually more complete approximations. What guides the learner is the desire to 'make sense' of the complexities of print with which he or she is confronted. For Ferreiro and Teberovsky, this is in tune with the actively constructivist view of learning of the Piagetian tradition to which they belong. For researchers such as Harste, Woodward and Burke (1984) such constructivism is rooted more in the social world within which 'reading' is an important act, but their conclusion is essentially the same. Schooling, in presenting the learning of reading as a task to be accomplished by the mastery of constituent activities, demands of children that they suspend their quest for making sense until they have achieved sufficient mastery of these activities. It is not surprising that, faced with this conflict between their intuitive understandings and the messages given by some of the most 'significant others' in their lives, some children sink into cognitive confusion. This may also, of course, be attributed to children's realisation that there is more to reading than simply guessing at the meanings of printed symbols with extensive help from the surrounding context. There may be a point in the learning of reading at which featural concepts loom much larger than functional concepts. Researchers such as Ehri (1991) have also argued that the context-bound learning of signs and symbols in a child's environment does not automatically transfer to the disembedded knowledge of the basis of these signs' composition (that is, using an alphabetically-based print system). Arguably, such disembedded knowledge is needed in order for the child to apply it to fresh stimuli. The challenge for teachers is to assist children's learning of the mechanics of print while helping them keep in mind an understanding of its functions.

It does seem to be the case that children who achieve more success at reading are those who show more balanced concepts of what the process is about, as suggested by a variety of studies such as those by Johns (1974) and Schneckner (1976). It may be that a wider awareness causes better reading, that successful reading leads to greater awareness or, as Ehri

(1979) hypothesises, awareness may interact with reading acquisition so that it is both a consequence of what has already occurred and a cause of further progress. In either case it seems that there are some children who, either because they are stronger in their convictions or more fortunate in their experience of teaching, make sufficient progress in reading to maintain their quest to 'make sense'.

(It should be noted that I am not suggesting that the conflict between children's pre-school literacy experiences and the underlying philosophy adopted during schooling is a cause of children not learning to read. The vast majority of children do learn to read very successfully at school. What may not be served well by schooling is their awareness of why and how they are doing this task.)

The implications for schooling of the strands of research reviewed in this chapter are fairly clear. If the development of positive and 'cognitively clear' perceptions of reading is seen as a suitable aim for teachers of the process (or skill, depending on the theoretical position from which one looks at it), then we need to take much more account of the perceptions and beliefs about reading which children develop before their schooling commences and, where these are positive, attempt to build upon them during their early school experience of reading teaching. This will mean concentrating upon the functions of reading before attending to its forms, that is, ensuring that school-reading experience starts from a basis of meaning and embeds work on constituent aspects, such as sound-symbol relationships, within this. This does not deny the fact, of course, that most children will need to be taught the alphabetic basis of English orthography. Some, but not the majority, will absorb this unconsciously through meaningful interactions with the print around them. Most will need to have it explicitly drawn to their attention, and sensitive teaching will involve doing this while maintaining the emphasis upon meaning which children bring from their interactions with print outside school. It may also mean giving explicit attention to a functional understanding of reading with those children who, for one reason or another, have lost sight of these insights and, consequently, may make little progress from simply being given 'more practice' at reading (Medwell, 1990a). A 'linguistically aware' approach to teaching does seem to have some basis, a conclusion which will resurface again and again in other chapters in this book.

3 *Awareness and the development of reading: syntax, sound and structure*

Introduction

There are wider areas of research which also have a bearing on the question of what young children know about reading, and in many ways these are informed by what is currently known about children's knowledge about language generally (see Chapter 1). Three areas of major importance will be discussed here: the awareness of syntax, the development of phonological awareness, and the awareness of the language and structure of books. In each of these, as mentioned in Chapter 2, one of the central questions concerns the sequence of acquisition of awareness and ability. Does the awareness precede and perhaps cause the ability, or is it a consequence of becoming able? It will quickly be seen that, in fact, this question is nowhere near as simple as it appears.

Syntactic awareness

It was suggested in Chapter 1 that an awareness of grammatical appropriateness begins to emerge at a fairly early stage in young children's development. The work of Clay (1972) and Weber (1970) was cited as evidence that young children tend to substitute words of the same part of speech when they make mistakes in oral reading. The work of Berko (1958) also suggests that young children have an awareness of the meaning-carrying parts of words (morphemes). Later studies, such as that by Pratt, Tunmer and Bowey (1984), have suggested that some forms of such syntactic awareness develop most extensively for the majority of children between the ages of 5 and 6. In their research, they read 5- and 6-year-old children sentences in which there were grammatical errors and asked the children to 'fix them up'. The errors were of two types: either word-order violations (for example, 'Teacher the read a story'), or morpheme omissions (for example, 'She ate Mary apple'). In the case of morpheme omissions, all the children were able to correct most sentences. It is true, however, that this does not necessarily imply awareness, since in these sentences the meaning was so obvious, and the urge in language users to make sense of what they hear is usually so strong, that the children may not even have noticed the errors. Bowey (1986) attempted to check for this in a later study by asking children to repeat verbatim deliberately incorrect sentences. Five year olds had great difficulty in doing this which, Bowey suggests, may indicate a lack of explicit awareness.

The word-order task in the Pratt, Tunmer and Bowey experiment was performed differently by the two age groups of children. The 6 year olds scored over 75 per cent correct 'fix ups', whereas the 5 year olds scored less than 50 per cent correct on average.

These findings suggest that at a certain stage in children's language careers the implicit awareness of grammatical structure which they have developed through becoming language users begins to become more explicit and amenable to conscious inspection. It cannot merely be a coincidence that at this stage of their careers children are beginning to learn to read. Through reading they are likely to be introduced to a richer variety of syntactic structures, wrestling with which should extend their awareness of syntax in general. Some support for this hypothesis comes from a study by Reid (1972). She took sentences from a range of reading material produced for 7 to 8 year olds which, however, she judged to be ambiguous and difficult in their syntactic structure. These sentences were rewritten to make them less ambiguous and the two versions were shown to 7-year-old children. These children were then asked questions about the sentence. Some examples of Reid's material are as follows:

Example 1

Original sentence: The girl standing beside the lady had a blue dress.

Modified sentence: The girl had a blue dress and she was standing beside the lady.

Question: Who had a blue dress?

Example 2

Original sentence: Tom's mother was anything but pleased.

Modified sentence: Tom's mother was not pleased at all.

Question: Was Tom's mother pleased?

In example 1, only 41 per cent of the children answered the question correctly after reading the original sentence. Eighty-eight per cent of those who read the modified sentence answered correctly. In example 2, the percentages of children making correct answers were 43 per cent for the original sentence and 80 per cent for the modified sentence.

Reid uses her findings to advocate that greater consideration needs to be given to the linguistic structures used in early reading material. She also suggests that children, especially those from particular family backgrounds, are put at a disadvantage when it comes to reading texts unless they have had a great deal of prior experience of being read aloud to from texts using similar structures. This suggestion receives support from other sources, as will be shown in a later section, but it is important to state at this point that there is an alternative conclusion to be drawn from Reid's results. It might be argued that, by being faced in their reading with syntactic structures which are new to them, and being required to come to terms with them, children might thereby expand their awareness of syntax and be able to use this to improve their reading in future. This argument would, of course, only apply under certain conditions. Children would need to be in a context in which they were motivated to come to terms with unfamiliar language patterns, which implies that their interest had been aroused by what they were reading. The enabling power of interesting material is reasonably well established (Asher, 1980). They would also need sympathetic guidance to help them overcome problems with the language of texts. This guidance may come from a more experienced reader using an apprenticeship model of learning to read, or from the author of the text itself who may provide support either from illustrations or textual means (Meek, 1988). These conditions coincide with the suggestions of Smith (1978) that, 'two basic necessities for learning to read are the availability of interesting material that makes sense to the learner and an understanding adult as a guide' (p. 7).

Whatever the strength of this argument, it does seem very likely that, in terms of an expansion of awareness about syntax, the single most important event for young children is beginning to learn to read. The sequence is, in effect, a circular one. Children develop an implicit awareness of grammatical structure from their interactions with other language users early in life. They apply this awareness to the task of reading, and their attempt to cope with this task both broadens their awareness of a range of structures and, at the same time, causes this awareness to become more explicit. This more explicit awareness enables them to tackle a wider range of structures in their reading which, in turn, expands the awareness.

Awareness and ability to read both influence each other, but to begin with it is the experience of reading which triggers the development.

Phonological awareness

A great deal of research interest has been generated quite recently by the issue of children's phonological awareness and the question of whether or not this plays an important part in learning to read. Peter Bryant and his colleagues at the University of Oxford have been largely responsible for bringing this work to the attention of a wide audience (Bryant and Bradley, 1985; Goswami and Bryant, 1990). Findings in this area have been used (and misused) by several exponents of phonic approaches to the teaching of reading as support for their position and deserve careful analysis.

Central to Bryant's argument is an understanding of just what is entailed in phonological awareness – awareness of the sounds which make up words. There are three ways of breaking up a word into constituent sounds and, therefore, three types of phonological awareness. First, words can be divided up into syllables. Most language speakers, including young children (Liberman, Shankweiler, Fischer and Carter, 1974), have little difficulty in separating the words *daddy, bungalow* and *magnificent* into two, three and four syllables respectively, and hence it can be argued that awareness of this type of phonological unit is early to emerge and quite well developed by the time children learn to read.

A second way of dividing up words, and thus a second type of phonological awareness, is by phonemes, that is, the smallest units of sound in words. The word *dog*, for example, has three phonemes, represented by the letters d, o and g. The word *church* also has three phonemes, but in this case these are each represented by letter strings (digraphs), ch, ur and ch. Advocates of phonics teaching methods lay great stress on children being taught the relationships between phonemes and the letter strings which can represent them, but the evidence suggests that young children are not actually aware of these sound units before they have had some experience of reading, as will be explained later.

The third way of dividing up words, which has provided a rich source of interest for current understanding of children's phonological awareness, looks at units larger than phonemes but smaller than syllables. Each syllable can be divided into an opening and an end section. For example, the word *throw* has one syllable but two distinct parts, thr and ow. In the word *chasing*, each syllable also has two parts, ch-a and s-ing. These units are referred to as the onset and the rime. The use of the term, rime, for the end units makes obvious reference to the fact that words which finish with similar rimes do rhyme. It is quite clear that rhymes are a very significant part of young children's lives. They are taught them and make up their own long before they start school (Dowker, 1989) and can detect rhyme and alliteration before they begin to read (Bradley and Bryant, 1983). Their experience of and sensitivity to rhymes seems to be closely linked to their fluency in reading and to their experience of nursery rhymes in their early years (Bryant, Bradley, MacLean and Crossland, 1989).

The three types of sound-related word divisions are shown in Table 3.1 (taken from Goswami and Bryant, 1990):

Table 3.1 The three types of sound-related word divisions

	SYLLABLE	ONSET AND RIME	PHONEMES
cat	cat	c-at	/c/a/t/
string	string	str-ing	/s/t/r/i/ng/
wigwam	wig-wam	w-ig w-am	/w/i/g/w/a/m/

Although there is plenty of evidence for a connection between children's reading and their awareness of sounds, this evidence does suggest that the direction of the connection is different for the different types of phonological awareness.

Research on Portuguese illiterates by Morais, Cary, Alegria and Bertelson (1979) found that these people were particularly bad at phonological tasks compared to a group of people who had been illiterate but had learned to read through an adult literacy programme. Learning to read seemed to have led to greater phonological awareness, rather than phonological awareness enabling the learning of reading. Similar conclusions can be drawn from studies of readers who learned to read with alphabetic (as in the case of English) or logographic scripts (as in the case of traditional Chinese or Japanese scripts). Read, Zhang, Nie and Ding (1986) compared people who had learnt to read with traditional Chinese logographic orthography with others who had learnt with an alphabetic version of Chinese script. The logographic script learners were much worse at phonological skills than the alphabetic script learners. Mann (1986) compared Japanese (logographic script learners) with American (alphabetic script learners) 6-year-old children. The two groups were similar in their awareness of syllables, but the American children were better at phoneme awareness tasks. It appears that it is learning to read with an alphabetic script that, in particular, leads to phonological skill.

Studies have also compared children before and after they began to learn to read. The original work of Bruce (1964), since confirmed many times, found that 5- and 6-year-old children had great difficulty with tasks which involved removing a sound from a word (for example, removing j from *jam*; n from *snail*; k from *fork*). Seven year olds did better, but it was not until 8 or 9 that children managed a reasonable performance. These children's abilities to manipulate phonemes did not begin to develop until they had made a start on learning to read. Studies such as that of Calfee (1977) and Content, Morais, Alegria and Bertelson (1982) have, however, subsequently suggested that children do better in this type of experiment when the sound they have to remove is the onset, leaving the rime intact.

Work with tapping tasks, where children have to tap for each sound they hear in spoken words, has found that young children can tap correctly for syllables but not for phonemes (Liberman, Shankweiler, Fischer and Carter, 1974). They tend to tap out the number of letters rather than the number of sounds (Tunmer and Nesdale, 1985), which suggests that their way into understanding phonemes is through the letters which stand for them. This again supports the idea that awareness of phonemes is a result of reading experience rather than a precursor.

There is, however, also evidence that an awareness of onset and rime develops fairly early. Kirtley, Bryant, MacLean and Bradley (1989) report an experiment in which 5, 6 and 7 year olds were given tasks which involved saying which was the odd word out of groups such as:

1   doll, deaf, can (the oddity is in the first phoneme and the onset);

2   mop, lead, whip (the oddity is in the last phoneme – a part of the rime);

3   top, rail, hop (the oddity is in the rime);

4   cap, doll, dog (the oddity is in the first two phonemes – crossing the onset/rime boundary).

Groups 1 and 3 (where onset and rime were preserved) were found much easier, with even children who could not read able to have some success. Groups 2 and 4 (where onset and rime were disrupted) were only found possible by children who had begun to read. Phoneme awareness seems,

therefore, to develop through learning to read, but some awareness of
onset and rime seems to be already present before reading begins.

This view of the development of phoneme awareness is supported by
evidence that beginning readers approach words without any analysis
of phoneme-grapheme relationships. This is an inconvenient conclusion
for those who advocate that teaching reading should begin by a focus
on sound-symbol relationships (a phonic approach), but not damning if
phonological awareness is conceived of as including onset and rime
sensitivity. Bryant and Bradley (1983) found that children beginning
reading seemed to adopt a visual strategy for the task, recognising words
as logograms. As they became more proficient at reading, they began
to use phonological coding rather more. This is further evidence that
reading causes phonological awareness rather than vice-versa.

The interesting question arises of how, if children use a visual strategy for
recognising words, can they manage to read new words? Giving children the
tools to do this has long been one of the major arguments in favour of a
phonics approach to reading teaching. Evidence suggests, however, that
children do this largely by making analogies. Goswami (1986) has shown
that even 5-year-old children who had not begun to read were able to
do this. Her experiment involved teaching children new words, such as
beak, and then asking them to read other words which shared spelling features
with the original word, either the same rime, for example *weak*, the same
onset and part of the rime, for example *bean*, or some of the same letters
in different orders, for example *lake*. It was found that children of 5, 6 and
7 years old all read words with the same rime better than the others, and
the difference was particularly marked in the case of the 5 year olds. Young
children also seem to be able to make analogies on the basis of onset.

This seems to suggest that as soon as children begin to learn to read they
do begin to adopt a phonological approach to the task, but that this is
based on the phonological units which make most sense to them – onset
and rime. Goswami (1990) also showed that there is a link between children's
sensitivity to rhyme and alliteration when they begin school and their
progress in learning to read over the following three years, even when
the effects of intelligence are controlled for.

This kind of evidence is used by Goswami and Bryant (1990) to suggest
a particular model for the development of reading in young children
and the role of phonological awareness within it. The model proposes that
children given experience of rhyme and alliteration develop an awareness of
these before they begin to learn to read. They actually begin reading using

only a visual approach to recognising w
of onset and rime allows them to apply
new words. Through experience of read
of the phonemic basis of alphabetic scrip
this new-found awareness. Phonological a
is therefore both a precursor to, and a proc
provides no support for an approach to the
around phonics drills, but it does suggest tha
classroom emphasis upon rhymes (nursery or
important than previously realised. There also   ⌐t for the
strategy of heightening beginning readers' awar   ⌐unds in words
by pointing these out to them. Traditional 'I-spy games and 'sound
tables', etc., do seem to make a valuable contribution, but what is most
significant from the point of view of this book is the fact that these activities
are designed actually to operate upon children's awareness rather than
simply upon their implicit knowledge.

Awareness of book language

According to Smith (1977), foremost among the insights a child needs in
order to learn to read is an awareness that written language obeys different
conventions to spoken language. Smith argues that approaching a written
text with expectations that it will behave in the same way and provide the
same kind of support as spoken language will not help the beginning
reader. An awareness of written language conventions is essential. Since,
by definition, children who cannot yet read cannot begin to develop this
awareness from reading themselves, it follows that they need to
experience written text and its structures and conventions in other ways.
The obvious way is through hearing written text read aloud.

This suggests that, in theory, there might be a link between children's
experience of hearing stories read aloud and their subsequent acquisition of
reading ability. The theory would predict that experience with stories
would develop understanding of story structures and familiarity with
the grammatical features and sequences of written language. These in turn
would enable subsequent anticipation of these structures and features which
would assist the reading of them (which does not, of course, mean that
there is no need for teaching children how to interpret features of written
language other than the structural). The proposition underlying this
theory, the link between hearing stories and becoming a proficient
reader, has received support from research and, indeed, it has been

...s the major way in which the particular expectations ...successfully with reading develop (Wells, 1987). If this is ...ry clear 'what no bedtime story means' (Heath, 1982). When ...do have this experience before they begin school, they seem much ...e likely to be able to 'talk like a book' (Clay, 1972), which in turn seems to be of critical value in becoming a competent reader.

Young children's awareness of the features of stories, from their stylistic conventions to the complex narrative rules around which they are based, has been investigated from several angles.

Fox (1988) has studied the oral narratives of young children and noted the influence upon these of experience with books. As an example of this, the following spoken narrative, produced by a 5-year-old boy, is taken from Fox's work.

> but then he went out in the middle of
> the night
> and there was this sound going – dooo-deedoo-dee [child
> sings]
> he looked all around
> nobody was there in a small street where
> it had lots of holes
> he looked down one of them
> he looked down the other
> they were all alike
> but he looked down the next one
> and what was there?
> just a surprise thing
> his Daddy was there

Clearly there is much more here than the simple narrating of an event. The child uses the story technique of building tension to engage his audience, and he phrases his narration in particular ways which owe more to written language rules than to spoken. The ability to do these things is evidence of a great deal of knowledge of the way stories work and the rules of written language.

Sulzby (1986) has examined the ways in which children import written language features into their speech by focusing on the 'reading intonation' they produce when talking about the picture in a book. In the language young children (who cannot yet read) produce when 'reading' a picture book, she found clear evidence of two forms of speech: one form which could be considered by a listener to be the text and which was modelled upon 'book language', and another which followed spoken language patterns and consisted of comments upon the text. This, she argues, is evidence for the early existence of metalinguistic awareness.

> In short, the children create a textual entity, separate from the rest of their speech, which they can comment upon and treat as an 'object'.
> (Sulzby and Otto, 1982, p. 193)

Fisher and Sommerwill (1990) analyse the way in which young children's writing, in its adoption of particular stylistic features and vocabulary, shows the influence of their reading.

The genesis of this understanding is traced by Snow and Ninio (1986) to early mother–child interactions with picture books, which appear to follow remarkably predictable routines (Ninio and Bruner, 1978). During the course of these interactions, children are initiated not only into book language, but also into several other literacy 'contracts', such as the facts that, in reading, the book leads and the reader is led, pictures represent things and events, and books operate outside of real time in an autonomous 'other' world. Snow and Ninio point out that reading books depends upon an understanding of these contracts, none of which have anything to do with children's independent deciphering of the words on the page. Such understanding is obviously not all that children need to know about in learning to read. As Tizard *et al.* (1988) conclude from their study of inner-city children, immersion in stories is a necessary but not sufficient condition for reading success. It needs to run hand in hand with systematic attempts to draw children's attention to the code by which print relates to meaning.

This last point notwithstanding, it does seem that there is a distinct relationship between children's experience of the style and structures of written language and their emergent use of these, in both speech and writing. Being able to talk and write 'like a book' leads also to an increasing ability to read book language, experience of which in turn increases the awareness of particular stylistic and structural conventions.

Conclusion

In each of the areas reviewed in this chapter, the relationship revealed between awareness and reading ability appears to be a cyclical one. Children come to the task of learning to read with particular experiences which have prepared them to varying degrees for the task. They use their awareness as a way in to reading, but the experience of learning to read is itself an important trigger to the development of a wider and more explicit awareness about the forms and features of printed language. This wider awareness in turn enables a greater mastery of the process of reading. Awareness and the ability to read are thus inextricably linked together to such an extent that it would be difficult to conceive of one developing in the absence of the other.

4 Awareness and the development of writing

Introduction

In many ways, the picture found when one examines the evidence concerning the awareness children have about the functions and forms of writing is similar to that discussed in Chapter 2, the awareness of the reading process, although it is based so far on much more limited evidence. The very few studies which have investigated the perceptions of writing held by children at school have tended to show that they are largely concerned with forms (spelling, neatness, accuracy, etc.), whereas studies of younger children carried out from an emergent literacy perspective have revealed a good deal of awareness of the functions of writing (as well as an emergent awareness of forms). Again, children's experience of schooling often seems to lead them to overemphasise form at the expense of function, with consequent negative effects in terms of their willingness to engage in writing and their attitudes towards it. This chapter will review some of the evidence concerning both school and pre-school children's perceptions of writing, and will go on to look at some possible causes for the apparent mismatch which is often found.

What do children think about writing?

Perhaps unsurprisingly, studies of children's perceptions of writing are vastly outnumbered by studies of perceptions of reading. This is largely explained by the general paucity of research in the writing area, which has only recently begun to attract serious interest from researchers. There is certainly a great need for further investigations, both small and large scale, into the perceptions and attitudes which primary children have towards an activity which, after all, seems to take up the lion's share of their attention at school. Research in progress at the University of Exeter (Wray, 1990; Medwell, 1990b) is beginning to suggest that the complete environment for writing which primary teachers try to provide for their pupils is filtered through these pupils' perceptions of what they are doing when they write. Thus, to understand and, perhaps, improve the context of classroom writing, it is necessary to understand pupils' perceptions.

I shall, therefore, after reviewing the small number of relevant studies already available, outline in greater detail a study recently carried out in conjunction with a group of teacher education students at the University of Exeter, which provided information about the perceptions of writing held by primary children of various ages.

Perceptions of writing: research evidence

The most substantial source of information about children's perceptions of writing is that provided during the course of the National Writing Project, and detailed in one of the several volumes finally published by this project (National Writing Project, 1990). Finding out what their pupils thought about writing emerged as a major concern for many of the teachers involved in the project and, to judge from the project's publications, especially its newsletter, the insights gained by these teachers as a result of this concern were among the more influential in affecting their views about writing. The evidence provided by the project is, however, problematic. Much of it is anecdotal and it was not gained under very controlled conditions and, while this is not a difficulty when the investigations it comes from are perceived as largely awareness-enhancers for the teachers carrying them out, it does make it difficult to accept the evidence as fully indicative of a general picture.

This reservation notwithstanding, the surveys carried out under the auspices of the project did seem to reveal a fairly general picture of perceptions of writing. This is summarised in one of the project publications (National Writing Project, 1990, p. 19) as a list of concerns identified by teachers:

- children often judge the success of their writing by its neatness, spelling and punctuation rather than by the message it conveys;

- children often have difficulty in talking about their own development as writers except in very broad terms;

- children see writers as people who publish books (usually stories); writing is thus thought about in terms of end products;

- writing is often seen as a school activity whose primary purpose is to show teachers what has been learnt;

- writing is seen as an individual activity; ideas for writing are rarely discussed and outcomes rarely shared with others;

- writing, talking and reading are not always clearly associated with each other.

These children were, therefore, apparently much more concerned with writing as a product than as a process, and as such their attention seemed to concentrate upon the appearance of that product, that is, its technical features, such as spelling and punctuation. This attention to product is not terribly surprising, of course. It is only in the last decade or so that educational researchers, stimulated by the pioneering work of Emig (1971) and Graves (1973), have begun to investigate the writing process, and teachers similarly have traditionally given much more attention to writing products than to processes.

The APU Language Monitoring surveys of 1979–83 (reported in Assessment of Performance Unit, 1988) support the tendency of primary children to foreground presentation, neatness and spelling. In response to the question, 'What do you think a good writer needs to know in order to do well?', over half the 11 year olds surveyed referred to transcription aspects of writing.

This primary attention to technical features is seen again in the results of a survey in West Cumbria primary schools reported in Martin, Waters and Bloom (1989). A group of 429 11-year-old children were asked, 'What is the first thing your teacher looks for when you hand in a piece of writing, such as a story?' The replies are shown in Table 4.1.

TABLE 4.1 Replies to questions, 'What is the first thing your teacher looks for when you hand in a piece of writing . . . ?'

Handwriting, neatness, presentation	42.2%
Spelling	25.4%
Punctuation and grammar	15.8%
Whether it makes sense and style	6.1%
Content	5.2%
Effort	0.9%
Length	0.6%
Planning	0.3%

Source: Martin, Waters and Bloom (1989).

The emphasis on writing as a product is very noticeable, but what is even more remarkable is the extreme concern (over 80 per cent of replies) with what are referred to in the National Curriculum documents as 'secretarial skills' (D.E.S., 1989); handwriting, neatness, presentation, spelling, punctuation and grammar. It is true, however, that the phrasing of the initial question in this study is such that it naturally focuses attention upon an end-product. When teachers look at completed pieces of writing, it must be difficult for children to realise that they might bear in mind the process by which this writing was produced. In addition, this question, and hence this study, are explicitly enquiring into what children think their teachers think about writing. This may not coincide with what the children themselves think about it.

The small-scale survey reported by Tamburrini, Willig and Butler (1984) of the conceptions of writing of 10- and 11-year-old children presents a less one-sided picture. These children were asked why they wrote stories, poems and project work in class. The responses were varied. In the case of stories, over half the sample mentioned 'developing the imagination' as the reason for the writing, while a similar proportion mentioned learning skills, such as spelling and handwriting. For poetry, a quarter mentioned learning skills as its purpose, while over half could think of no purpose at all. As for project work, over three-quarters gave learning facts as the purpose, which does suggest a greater realisation of writing functions.

American research into this area, however, tends to confirm the picture of children preoccupied with secretarial aspects and writing products. Hogan (1980) surveyed 13,000 children aged between 8 and 14 and found that children's interest in writing appeared to decline as they got older. A similar picture emerged in the report of the National Assessment of Educational Progress (1980) with the number of children who said they enjoyed writing dropping by half between the ages of 9 and 13. Shook, Marrion and Ollila (1989) suggest that a possible explanation for this is that, 'Students may be sacrificing self-expression while being hopelessly tangled in mechanics, because educators have unwittingly trivialised writing' (p. 133).

Shook *et al.* (1989) surveyed the concepts of writing held by over a hundred children aged between 6 and 8. The children were asked questions relating to three general categories: their perceptions of the general purpose for writing; their personal preferences about writing, and their self-concepts as writers. The results indicated that:

- The children understood the communicative nature of writing and perceived that it was an important activity in the world outside school.

- Most children reported doing more writing at home than at school and getting more help with their writing from people at home than from their teachers.

- Most saw themselves as needing more practice, better equipment or neater printing in order to become better writers, that is, mechanical aspects.

- Over three-quarters, when asked why they wrote at school, responded with reasons relating to mechanical aspects, such as to learn more words and letters, to practise, because teacher says so. Only a fifth said they wrote because it was fun.

The researchers conclude, among other things, that their survey suggests a difference between children's experiences of writing at home and at school in terms of ownership. At home the children set their own purposes for writing and sought help in meeting these purposes: purposes and help both relating to writing as a means of communicating meaning. At school children tended to write because their teachers told them to and were, therefore, in danger of losing a sense of ownership of their writing. Following from this they tended to become concerned about aspects other than communication, and the mechanics of writing began to loom larger as objects for attention.

A survey of primary children's thoughts about writing

Because of the scarcity of hard evidence concerning primary children's views about writing, a study was conducted with the assistance of a group of students engaged in a Postgraduate Certificate in Education course at the University of Exeter. Each student collected written comments about writing from up to ten children, aged between 7 and 11 years. From a group of 58 students, writing from 475 children was collected, made up as shown in Table 4.2.

TABLE 4.2 Writings collected by PGCE students at Exeter University

Group 1	aged 7/8	112 pieces of which 90 were useful
Group 2	aged 8/9	105 pieces (93)
Group 3	aged 9/10	141 pieces (140)
Group 4	aged 10/11	117 pieces (117)

In carrying out the study, the first important decision to be made concerned the exact nature of the task which would be given to the children. Simply to ask them, 'What do you think about writing in school?' did not seem adequate for a number of reasons. First, this question is fairly abstract in nature and, as was suggested in Chapter 2, asking children abstract questions is unlikely to yield meaningful responses. Secondly, because the people asking these children the questions were at the time involved in teaching them, there was a danger that children would tend to tailor their responses to fit what they believed these teachers wished to hear, a not uncommon problem in teacher research. Thirdly, it was felt that asking the question in as open-ended a way as this may lead to a rather amorphous set of replies, whereas what was really needed was to tap into what these children considered the most important aspects of writing in their classes.

With these considerations in mind, it was decided to frame the task in a more concrete way. This was done by using a modified form of the task used in the International Study of Written Composition (Bauer and Purves, 1988) partly to assess the opinions about writing of students at or near the end of compulsory schooling in 14 different countries. (The results of this study have not yet been published.) In the international study, the task was phrased as follows:

> Write a letter of advice to a student two years younger than you who is planning to attend your school and who has asked you to tell them how to write a composition that will be considered good by teachers in your school. Write a friendly letter and describe in it at least five specific hints as to what you think teachers in your school find important when they judge compositions.

With somewhat younger children, the task in the present study was phrased as:

Someone in the class below yours has asked you what the
writing will be like when he/she comes into your class. Write
and tell him/her, and try to give him/her some useful advice
about what he/she will have to do to do good writing in
your class.

All the children in the study were given the task in more or less these
words, and their subsequent writing collected. In terms of producing
extended statements from these children, the task seemed to work very
well, with only 35 pieces, mainly from the younger two age groups, being
too short to give any useful information.

The results of the study can be approached in either a quantitative or a
qualitative way, with both giving useful information. A straight count
of the features of writing mentioned by the children produced the figures
shown in Table 4.3.

TABLE 4.3 Survey results: primary children's thoughts about writing

FEATURES	GROUP 1 (aged 7–8 years)	GROUP 2 (aged 8–9 years)	GROUP 3 (aged 9–10 years)	GROUP 4 (aged 10–11 years)
Spelling	22.99	21.56	20.56	16.43
Neatness	18.58	21.89	17.87	13.00
Length	14.56	11.44	15.89	9.77
Punctuation	13.22	10.45	9.46	10.63
Tools	7.47	12.77	5.14	
Layout	3.07	2.82	1.17	0.32
Secretarial	79.89	80.93	70.09	50.16
Words	6.90	4.64	6.78	9.77
Ideas	8.43	8.96	12.73	16.33
Structure	1.15	1.99	4.79	7.84
Characters		1.49	2.34	7.63
Style			0.82	5.69
Composition	16.48	17.08	27.45	47.26

Spelling, the most frequently mentioned feature in all age groups, would usually be referred to by phrases such as 'Make sure you get your spellings right' or 'Use a dictionary to spell words you don't know'. Neatness would be referred to by things such as 'Do your best handwriting' or 'Make sure it is not messy'. Many children stressed that the writing had to be 'long enough', although a significant number warned not to make it too long 'because Miss might get bored'. Both types of comment are included under the length category. Under 'punctuation' are included mentions of the need for full stops and capital letters, commas and speech marks. The category 'tools' refers to the surprisingly frequent mention of the materials with which to write, such as 'make sure your pencil is sharp' or 'Mr Ellis gets cross if you do not use a ruler to underline the title', while under 'layout' are included references to the drawing of a margin or the placing of the date, etc. Some children referred to the importance of 'words' as, for example, in 'Don't use the same word over and over again', while others referred to 'ideas' as in 'Try to have some funny bits' or 'Stories should be interesting and exciting'. A few mentioned 'structure', as, for example, in 'A story needs a beginning, a middle and an end', a few 'characters', as in 'Write about interesting people', and even fewer 'style', as in 'In poems you can repeat words to make it sound good' or 'Don't begin sentences with "and"'.

The figures recorded under the heading 'secretarial' in the table are derived from adding those under 'spelling', 'neatness', 'length', 'punctuation', 'tools' and 'layout', while those under 'composition' are derived from the adding of 'words', 'ideas', 'structure', 'characters' and 'style'. These give an idea of the balance of children's preoccupations in writing at the various ages.

In interpreting this table, the first thing to state is the problematic nature of the methods of enquiry. Although the task the children were asked to do is less abstract than the straightforward question, 'What is writing?', it is still impossible to assume that the children's answers reflected entirely their real concepts about writing. The methodological problems involved in trying to tap children's concepts about such 'taken for granted' activities as writing were discussed in Chapter 2 in the context of reading. It is quite possible that the children's statements reflect not what they really think about writing, but what they think their teacher wants them to think. Even at this level, however, the results may tell a good deal about what counts as important in writing in these children's classrooms, about which children are usually most perceptive.

The results show an overwhelming preoccupation with the secretarial aspects of writing among the younger three age groups. Only in the older group does there appear to be a balance of concern between secretarial and composition aspects. In all groups, spelling is the most frequently mentioned feature, followed quite closely in the youngest three groups by neatness. Features such as characters and style are barely mentioned by children younger than 10 and, while ideas and structure do receive some attention from the younger children, this does not begin to be substantial until the age of 9 or so. There is an interesting peaking of attention to neatness and tools among the 8/9 year olds, both of which fade in importance, tools entirely so, by 10/11. This is perhaps due to the traditional transition to 'joined up writing' and the use of pens rather than pencils which takes place around the second year junior stage.

It should not be assumed, of course, that these statements of children's explicit preoccupations in writing relate to their actual abilities to handle the features mentioned in their writing. Two examples will be sufficient to highlight the dangers in making assumptions like this. Two of the least-mentioned features, especially in the younger groups, were structure and characters. However, Kroll and Anson (1984) have shown that attention to story structure is evident in the story writing of 9 year olds. They suggest that, in the same way that, through exposure to large numbers of stories, children 'acquire internalised expectations about story structure which guide their understanding and remembering of narratives' (p. 157), children also acquire internalised models which guide their creation of stories. There is evidence that many beginning writers can produce stories which show some awareness of basic narrative structure in that they include settings, characters and events (Temple, Nathan and Burris, 1982) using the basic story grammar terminology of Mandler and Johnson (1977). Similarly, Fox (1990) has shown that most children between the ages of 7 to 8 and 10 include interacting characters in their narrative, albeit with limited realisation of the inner psychological worlds of these characters. Although young children can handle these features to a certain extent in their writing, they seem not, according to the results of this study, to be particularly 'aware' of them.

In looking qualitatively at the results of the study, it is interesting to look in detail at individual responses. The fullest statements of the study came from two 10-year-old girls (incidentally from the same classroom). These are reproduced in typed form (with original spellings and punctuation) overleaf.

Piece 1

I enjoy writing in the junior class and I think that when the little ones go up to a higher class to make their work more exciting they should use their imagination and they should express their words such as instead of saying . . . I saw a nice bird on a branch, put I saw a pigeon sitting on a branch of a oak tree in the woods. Also they should learn to spell and put capitals in the right place. And before you take your work up to be marked you should always check it through and don't rush it. When you do come up in the juniors if you don't know who to spell something either ask the teacher or look in the dictionary. Sometimes its easier to split the word into two that way its a lot easier. Anyway thats enough about spelling. If you are writing a poem you don't just set it out normally, for example

Watch out watch out Jack Frost is about, He nibbles your toes and ears.

As well as that if your writing you should express how you feel, and do your ideas first. And don't always try to make it rhyme, because sometimes it doesn't make sense anyway thats just some of the rules about writing. Heres another one dont worry its short. The teachers sometimes say, I before E except after C. Well they do here anyway. Thats what I think.

Piece 2

In the junior class when writing it is better to express your words such as, instead of saying I saw a pretty flower, put, I saw a beautiful flower that blew from side to side in the wind. In the juniors we normally write adventure or fantasy storys about witches and wizards. When you get old enough you will be able to use big words, instead of little, very small, instead of big, enormouse. And it is a good idea before you get to old to try and write neatly joined up, it is good for letters when you are older, and may come in handy if you want to be a secatary. Example: the wind blew [printed]: → The wind blew strongly [cursive script]. When you get around 2nd or third year it is old enough for you to start looking in the dictionary for to express your words, as I said at the begining. It is old enough for you to stop going to the teacher and asking for words. And a few hints for people who are just starting the juniors: If you are stuck on a word, carry on writing, write what you think instead of getting up 30 times when writing a story, let the teacher correct them when you have finished, and if stuck on a word when reading, sound the letters out one by one. It is fun writing in the juniors.

Both these pieces are characterised by the very balanced views about writing which they express. They both mention secretarial features, but these are set firmly into an overall impression of the primacy of composition. Both begin by mentioning ideas and expression but go on to give excellent advice about spelling which many teachers of lower juniors would be very grateful if their children heeded.

These can be contrasted with the following two pieces, both produced by 9 year olds, which were much more typical in the study overall:

Piece 3

1. at the start of a sentence you have to put a capital letter.

2. if you are writing names you put a capital letter as well.

3. and in youre story book you do youre bets writing.

4. at the end of a sentence you put a full stop.

5. you have to write to tell storys and to tell people whate you have been doing

6. you can lern how to do joind-up writing like abcdefghijklmnopqrstuvwxyz [cursive script].

Piece 4

frist you put your pencle down and coppey a letter what someone put down like you are darwing make your big letters go up to the line above. put capitals letters at the bigan of centens and full stop at the end. get on with your work. if you doing story's don't let it cary on to long. don't make to much smches and used rubbers to much do your comers and speach mark's do your marging and don't wander about.

Here the children's major preoccupations are clearly with secretarial features. Composition barely figures at all. In piece 4 it is almost possible to hear the voice of this child's teacher, which in many ways is the chief message from this study. Whatever these children 'really' think about writing, what they have expressed are their feelings about what counts as being successful at writing in their classrooms and this, of course, is largely defined by their teachers. There were some rare examples of children expressing a tension between the messages about writing they glean from their classroom experiences and the understandings which seem to come from wider experiences of literacy use. The following piece, from a 10-year-old girl, shows quite well the clash between her understanding of the functions of writing outside school, and her assessment of its importance within school.

> *Piece 5*
>
> When you come up into Class 1 don't worry about the state of your writing we don't do much but I'll give you a few tips. Writing is information and is cheeper than phoneing Russia. The world would be pretty boring if there was no writing, you woulden't be able to read books you woulden't know about the worlds history or anything like that. My speling is atroshas it is slowly getting better thanks to the computers spelling list. I hate writing but I like reading a lot.

Pieces such as this show very well the importance for teachers of understanding how their pupils think and feel about writing and, perhaps, acting upon this information.

Young children's knowledge about writing

Nevertheless, as in the case of reading, the evidence which has come from researchers working from an emergent literacy perspective suggests a much more thorough awareness of writing functions and forms in young children than might be suspected on the basis of studies such as the one described above. The emphasis in emergent literacy research has been on what children can show that they know, rather than on what they seem not to understand. It is true, however, that researchers in this tradition tend to make assumptions about links between children's competence and their implicit awareness of what they are doing, and to underplay the role of explicit awareness in literate performances.

It may be useful at this point to give a statement of just what an emergent literacy perspective entails, before briefly reviewing some of the very influential research which has stemmed from it, particularly into young children's writing development. A convenient way of providing this is to quote the six research-based conclusions about early literacy development which Teale and Sulzby (1986) suggest underpin the new paradigm of emergent literacy. These are:

1   Literacy development begins before formal instruction starts. Children use a variety of reading and writing behaviours in the informal contexts of family and community.

2   Reading and writing develop concurrently, insights into the one continually informing the other. To understand these developments it is necessary to conceptualise the process as 'literacy development'.

3   Literacy develops in real life for real purposes. Literacy development is thus as much to do with learning about the functions of literacy as with learning the forms.

4   Cognitive activities which occur before schooling are an essential part of literacy learning.

5   Children learn literacy through engaging with literate adults in a literate world. Social interaction with significant adults is crucial in this, as is individual experimentation and hypothesis generation/testing/reformulation.

6   Although there are recognisable stages through which children's literacy learning passes, individuals can go through these stages in a number of ways and at a number of ages. Instruction needs to be responsive to this variation.

Based upon, and providing support for, these tenets, several major pieces of research have provided us with a good deal of information about early writing development. The work of Ferreiro and Teberovsky (1983) with Argentinian pre-schoolers shows children learning to write (and read) by making a continual series of hypotheses about the workings of the system, testing these out by writing, and refining, abandoning, and re-inventing their ideas about the production of written symbols. Arguing from a Piagetian perspective which sees learning as a process of interaction with, and action upon, the object of the learning, they show convincingly that the children they studied were not passively acquiring knowledge about writing but were, rather, actively constructing it for themselves. In other words, their learning was accomplished by conscious thought: awareness was inextricably embedded in the learning process.

The research of Harste, Woodward and Burke (1984) similarly shows young children actively involved in the construction of their own knowledge about literacy processes. This work is significant in that it adds a social dimension to an understanding of the process. The researchers see literacy as essentially a social practice, and children learning it are doing so as participants in social dialogue. They also present a picture of children's emergent literate behaviour as strategic, that is, there are a number of strategies which children adopt in the process of solving the problem that is literacy learning. As a strategic activity, literate behaviour involves for the child, as it does for an adult, selection between a range of possible actions. Selection involves choice, and choice implies that the chooser is acting with a degree of conscious awareness of the alternatives.

As an example of the way an emergent literacy researcher might examine the knowledge about writing of a young child, I shall examine a piece of 'emergent' writing. The piece in question (Figure 4.1) was produced by a 4-year-old girl, Sarah, who wrote it as a letter to Father Christmas asking for some presents. She read it back as, 'Dear Father Christmas, please can I have a Cindy doll and a bike. Love from Sarah'.

When examining the piece, it is tempting to concentrate first of all upon what Sarah does not know about writing. What she produces clearly does not conform to adult standards of writing, and is deficient in several ways – in letter formation, letter group to word correspondence, uniformity of letter size and shape, for example. There are ways, however, in which Sarah demonstrates in her writing that she has a great deal of understanding about the nature and the production of writing.

First, she shows clearly that she understands the purpose of writing is communication. She began with a need to communicate and something to say. She knew that an appropriate way of achieving her aim was to produce a series of marks on a piece of paper. She also knew that these marks had to bear a relationship to a spoken message, and had no hesitation in 'reading' what she had written. In her reading she showed a recognition that the particular message she wanted to communicate needed a particular format, and her message follows the accepted letter format of salutation, message, closure and signature.

Secondly she shows an awareness that writing requires a particular organisation. This knowledge is so familiar to adults that we tend to

Figure 4.1 Letter by Sarah, a 4-year-old girl

take it for granted. While watching Sarah write, however, it was very noticeable that she went about her task in an organised manner which she must have learnt from somewhere. She began her writing in the top left-hand corner of the page, and then proceeded to make her marks from left to right and top to bottom. Her marks follow clear line-like patterns. These features are clearly culturally specific (Chinese or Arabic children would presumably begin to write differently), but it is most unlikely that they have been deliberately taught to Sarah. Yet she knows their importance.

Thirdly Sarah demonstrates a feature which is very common in young children's first attempts at writing: a willingness to play with letter shapes – to experiment. She does not have at her command all the letters that she requires for her message, so she does the best she can with what she has. The letters she knows are, by and large, those that make up her name (even though her 'h' is reversed and her 'a' is similar to 'o'), so she uses these for her message, trying out different sizes as she does so. Her first line gets progressively higher, and she indicates by a line that she knows this.

These three features of communication, organisation and experimentation are commonly seen in the writing of young children (Newman, 1984), and demonstrate that, in fact, they have already probably learnt more about writing than they have left to learn. What is left is really refinement upon the basic features they have already mastered. But, most importantly from the point of view of the present book, they suggest that young children have thoughtful and balanced concepts of writing. Emergent literacy research presents us with a picture of young children actively engaged in constructing their own knowledge about writing (and literacy in general), not simply physically, but also cognitively. Learning to write is a thinking process and, therefore, an awareness of what one is doing, no matter how contextually embedded that may be, is an essential component of the process.

Form, function and schooling

As was the case in our discussion of children's knowledge about reading in Chapter 2, we are left with the task of explaining the apparent discrepancy between young children's meaning and social practice-centred ideas about writing and their older counterparts' seemingly overwhelming preoccupation with the technicalities of putting pencil to paper. As with reading, this can partially be explained by the simple fact that there is a great deal to learn about the technical aspects of writing and a feeling on the part of teachers that the learning of these things can be speeded up by giving the technical aspects direct attention. The problem with this is that children often begin to perceive the secretarial aspects as being extremely important to their teachers and, therefore, as teachers are the people who know best, necessarily of prime importance to the children themselves. They concentrate upon forms to the detriment of a developing awareness of functions.

This foregrounding of form in the teaching of writing can happen despite the teachers' best intentions. Medwell (1990b) relates a classroom observation which will be guiltily familiar to many primary teachers. The teacher had spent a considerable time discussing the topic of pirates with her class of 8 year olds. They had talked about the possibilities for writing about this exciting topic, and the teacher had exhorted them to write 'really exciting stories', that is, she had emphasised the function of the writing task. Yet, once they began to write their stories, every subsequent interaction between teacher and children was concerned with secretarial aspects. The teacher wrote spellings in their word books, wrote the occasional word on the board, commended some children for their neat writing and admonished others for their less than neat writing, etc. From an experience like this, which is likely to have been repeated several times, the children eventually get the message that, whatever the teacher says he or she is interested in, what he or she is really concerned about are spellings, neatness, etc.

Yet it is clear to children as well as adults that, in the world outside school, writing is produced and is read for a purpose. Function is pre-eminent and, while some attention is given to form (most people react badly to spelling mistakes in others' public writing, for example), nobody ever claims that the reason they are writing a note, letter, claim form, telephone number, etc. is to practise their spelling and handwriting. Indeed, in some of these examples, it is common for the writers to make very light of the fact that their writing may be virtually unreadable to anyone other than themselves. It is also quite common for liberties to be taken with form in the interests of better meeting the function of a piece of writing. The makers of 'Weetabix', 'Kleenex' and 'Kit-Kat' know that their sales are not going to be adversely affected by their unconventional spelling, but are more likely to be helped by their writing achieving its function by being positively identified with their product.

It seems that it is only in the world of schools that form in writing has such pre-eminence over function. There is a very powerful argument for redressing the balance in this area by trying to ensure that writing in school is truly purposeful and is seen to be so by the children. This involves a consideration of the possible purposes for writing and some thought about the provision of real audiences. It also seems to imply that teachers themselves must become more aware of their desired and actual roles as teachers of writing, and one of the most important of these roles should be to ensure that their pupils are fully *aware* of why, how, what and for whom they are writing.

5 Awareness and the understanding of reading

Introduction

While reading some particularly densely-written background material before writing this chapter, I noticed that it was becoming increasingly difficult for me to concentrate on what I was reading. My mind kept drifting to other, lighter topics, and several times I came to with a jerk to realise that I had understood nothing of the several paragraphs I thought I had 'read'. In the language around which this chapter will be based, this was a metacognitive experience, and my comprehension monitoring had alternately lapsed and kicked into action. These terms are probably unfamiliar to many people, yet the processes to which they refer have been increasingly demonstrated to be of special importance in intellectual development and in the operation of many intellectual activities, in particular, that of reading. This chapter will explore the areas of metacognition and reading, focusing in particular upon comprehension monitoring. The major part of the chapter will review the extensive and varied research into these areas and attempt to summarise its major findings and implications. First, though, I shall attempt to clarify the use of the terms themselves by exploring some definitions, thus laying the background for a discussion of the operation and importance of comprehension monitoring in reading.

Metacognition and comprehension monitoring

Vygotsky (1962) suggested that there are two stages in the development of knowledge: first, its automatic unconscious acquisition (we learn things or to do things, but do not know that we know these things) and, secondly, a gradual increase in active conscious control over that knowledge (we begin to know what we know and that there is more that we do not know). This distinction is essentially the difference between the cognitive and metacognitive aspects of knowledge and thought. The term 'metacognition' is used to refer to the deliberate conscious control of one's own cognitive actions (Brown, 1980). One of the most significant researchers responsible for our increasing knowledge about the phenomenon of metacognition has been the psychologist, Flavell, and his definition of it will serve as a good starting point for a more extended discussion of the concept and its relation to reading comprehension:

> Metacognition refers to one's knowledge concerning one's own cognitive processes and products or anything related to them, e.g. the learning-relevant properties of information or data. For example, I am engaging in metacognition . . . if I notice that I am having more trouble learning A than B; if it strikes me that I should double-check C before accepting it as a fact; if it occurs to me that I had better scrutinize each and every alternative in any multiple-choice type task situation before deciding which is the best one; if I sense that I had better make a note of D because I may forget it; . . . Metacognition refers, among other things, to the active monitoring and conscious regulation and orchestration of these processes in relation to the cognitive objects or data on which they bear, usually in the service of some concrete goal or objective.
> (Flavell, 1976, p. 232)

Metacognition is, therefore, essentially cognition about cognition: thinking about thinking. If cognition involves perceiving, understanding and remembering and so on, then metacognition involves thinking about one's own perception, understanding and memory (Garner, 1987).

It has been suggested that there is a hierarchical relationship between the terms 'metacognition', 'cognitive monitoring' and 'comprehension monitoring' (Baker and Brown, 1984). Metacognition can be seen as the wider concept; both metacognition and cognitive monitoring apply to knowledge about cognition in general. Comprehension monitoring is seen as applying mainly to the comprehension of connected discourse, which may involve either reading or listening (Wagoner, 1983). In thinking about this topic, the following kinds of questions tend to get asked (Wagoner, 1983). What do readers know about their own comprehension, that is, what they comprehend and how they comprehend? Are they aware of when they comprehend adequately and when they do not? How do readers decide when their comprehension is adequate? What kinds of strategies do readers use when they realise they are not comprehending what they read in order to compensate for this?

The remainder of this chapter will attempt to suggest some answers
to these questions, based upon the insights that have been gleaned
from research, but first it is useful to outline a distinction which has
proved useful in all metacognition research: 'Metacognition can be
differentiated into metacognitive knowledge and metacognitive experience'
(Flavell, 1981, p. 38). This distinction gives us two distinct areas of activities:
knowledge about cognition and the regulation of cognition.

It has been suggested by Baker and Brown (1984) that metacognitive
knowledge is the relatively stable information that we have about our
own thinking, and reading, processes. This knowledge may be about
ourselves, about the tasks we are faced with and about possible strategies
for tackling them. I may know, for example, that I have to read things at
least twice before I will understand them, that it is much easier to understand
texts if they are about a topic about which I already know something, or
that it will help me to remember information if I jot down key points
as I read them (Garner, 1987). The division into knowledge about person,
tasks and strategies has been a useful conceptual device underpinning
several research investigations in the area, as will be seen later.

This cluster of activities is concerned with a person's knowledge about
their own cognitive resources and the adequacy of these for particular tasks.
As we shall see later, to reflect on your own thinking processes, to be
aware of the way you go about reading, is a relatively late-developing skill
with important implications for children's effectiveness as active learners
from text (Baker and Brown, 1984).

The second cluster of activities are the mechanisms used by active learners
as they regulate their own attempts to solve problems. These might include:

- checking the outcome of what has already been attempted;

- planning the next moves in response to a problem;

- monitoring the effectiveness of these attempted actions;

- testing, revising and evaluating strategies for learning.

Although it has been demonstrated that even quite young children can
monitor their own activities when working on a simple problem (Brown,
1978), learners of any age are more likely to take active control of their
own cognitive activities when they are faced with tasks of medium
difficulty. This is unsurprising since it seems logical that with an easy task
there is no need to devote too much attention to it, and with a task
which is too hard there is a tendency to give up (Baker and Brown, 1984).

In terms of reading, this cluster of activities includes the strategies readers use to recognise and compensate for failures in comprehension. How do I know I have not understood a text, and what can I do about it when I know? Strategies of this kind are at the heart of the concept of comprehension monitoring, and it is this concept that I analyse in the following section.

Comprehension monitoring in reading

An analysis of the operation of comprehension monitoring during the reading process must begin with a description of what this process involves. Good reading has been described as follows:

> A good reader proceeds smoothly and quickly as long as his understanding of the material is complete. But as soon as he senses that he has missed an idea, that the track has been lost, he brings smooth progress to a blinding halt. Advancing more slowly, he seeks clarification in the subsequent material, examining it for the light it can throw on the earlier trouble spot. If still dissatisfied with his grasp, he returns to the point where the difficulty began and rereads the section more carefully. He probes and analyses phrases and sentences for their exact meaning; he tries to visualise abstruse descriptions; and through a series of approximations, deductions, and corrections he translates scientific and technical terms into concrete examples. (Whimbey, 1975, p. 91)

While it is, of course, true that all readers do not follow precisely this sequence of actions, recent theories of reading have suggested similar strategic models for the comprehension process. The model proposed by Ruddell (1976), for example, includes an evaluation of the adequacy of incoming information; it sees reading as a complex process involving data-gathering, hypothesis building, organising and synthesising data, and hypothesis testing. Goodman (1976) claims that readers test their hypotheses against the 'screens' of meaning and grammar by frequently asking themselves if what they are reading makes sense. The reader must 'monitor his choices so he can recognise his errors and gather more cues when needed' (p. 483). In fact, most characterisations of the reading process include skills and activities which involve what is now termed 'metacognition'. According to Brown (1980), some of the metacognitive activities involved in reading are:

1   clarifying one's purposes for reading, that is, understanding the explicit and implicit demands of a particular reading task;

2   identifying the important aspects of a text;

3   focusing attention on these principal aspects rather than on relatively trivial aspects;

4   monitoring ongoing activities to determine whether comprehension is taking place;

5   engaging in self-questioning to check whether the aims are being achieved;

6   taking corrective action if and when failures in comprehension are detected.

Reading for meaning therefore inevitably involves the metacognitive activity of comprehension monitoring, which entails keeping track of the success with which one's comprehension is proceeding, ensuring that the process continues smoothly and taking remedial action if necessary. It thus involves the use of what have been called 'debugging' skills (Brown, 1980).

Although mature readers typically engage in comprehension monitoring as they read for meaning, it is usually not a conscious experience. Brown (1980) distinguishes between an automatic and debugging state. Skilled readers, she argues, tend to proceed on automatic pilot until a 'triggering event' alerts them to a failure or problem in their comprehension. When alerted in this way, they must slow down and devote extra effort in mental processing to the area which is causing the problem. They employ debugging devices and strategies, all of which demand extra time and mental effort. Anderson (1980) suggests that efficient readers need not devote constant attention to evaluating their own understanding, and he suggests the existence of an 'automated monitoring mechanism' which 'renders the clicks of comprehension and clunks of comprehension failure'. This mechanism is sometimes referred to as the 'executive' (Garner, 1987), and is usually given credit for slowing down and allocating extra processing capacity to cognitive problem areas, that is, 'debugging' the problem, which requires turning off the 'automatic pilot' that characterises skilled performance.

The events that trigger such action may vary widely. One common triggering event is the realisation that an expectation held about a text has not been confirmed by actual experience of the text. For example, in reading a sentence such as the following: 'The old man the boats', the fourth and fifth words will probably cause a revision of the reader's sense of understanding and, therefore, take longer to process. Another triggering event is the meeting of unfamiliar ideas at too rapid a frequency for the reader to maintain a tolerance for the subsequent lack of understanding. The usual reader reaction to this is to slow down the rate of processing, devoting time and effort to the task of sorting out the failure in comprehension. The reader enters a deliberate, 'aware' state quite distinct from the automatic pilot state and the smooth flow of reading abruptly changes (Baker and Brown, 1984).

Realising that one has failed to understand is only part of comprehension monitoring; one must also know what to do when such failures occur. This involves the making of a number of strategic decisions. The first of these is simply to decide whether or not remedial action is required. This seems to depend largely upon the reader's purposes for reading (Alessi, Anderson and Goetz, 1979). For example, if a reader's purpose is to locate a specific piece of information, a lack of understanding of the surrounding text will not usually trigger any remedial action. On the other hand, if the purpose is to understand a detailed argument, then practically any uncertainty will spark off extra mental activity.

In the event of a decision to take action, there are a number of options available. The reader may simply store the confusion in his or her memory as an unanswered question (Anderson, 1980) in the hope that the author will subsequently provide sufficient clarification to enable its resolution; or the reader may decide to take action immediately, which may involve re-reading, jumping ahead in the text, consulting a dictionary or knowledgeable person, or a number of other strategies (Baker and Brown, 1984).

The occurrence of this range of strategies has been studied by Winser (1988), who asked readers of various ages to think aloud as they tried to understand difficult texts. The strategies they used when they encountered comprehension difficulties included the following:

- *reading on*: reading more of the text to see if more information could be gained;

- *sounding out*: examining letters and sounds carefully (this strategy was used most often by younger readers);

- *making an inference*: guessing a meaning on the basis of textual clues and previous knowledge;

- *re-reading*: reading the difficult section again;

- *suspending judgement*: waiting to see if the text provided more clues.

Having established what comprehension monitoring in reading involves, I shall now survey some of the research studies which have begun to give us a fairly complete picture of how it operates in various groups.

Research on comprehension monitoring in action

Because the area of comprehension monitoring has generated so much research interest over the last decade, especially in the USA, it is impossible to review all of this research in the space available. I shall therefore concentrate on what seem to be the most significant studies and shall divide the review into three sections. I shall, first, review the work which has examined comprehension monitoring in adult, fluent readers, which has largely meant undergraduate students. Secondly, I shall deal with the important pilot work in the area of listening comprehension, before, finally, discussing the picture we now have from research into the comprehension monitoring abilities of learner readers. Good, extensive reviews of all these areas are available elsewhere (Baker and Brown, 1984; Wagoner, 1983), that given by Garner (1987) being particularly extensive.

Studies involving undergraduate students

Two important studies of the comprehension monitoring of undergraduate students have given us insights into how this operates in mature, skilful readers. Baker (1979) gave students passages to read in which the middle paragraph had deliberately confusing features, such as inconsistent information, an unclear reference and inappropriate connecting words. A large proportion of these confusions (62 per cent) seemed not to be detected by the students even after they had been asked specifically to search for them. However, asking them afterwards about what they had been thinking while reading suggested that many of their failures to report confusions were due to their use of 'fix-up' strategies for resolving comprehension problems. They often, for example, made inferences from what they read in order to make up for the omission of information in the passage. With other text problems, they seemed to make a rapid assessment that the problem was unimportant and then ignored it.

Baker and Anderson (1982), also working with undergraduate students, used a computer terminal to present texts for evaluation. Passages containing inconsistencies were presented one sentence at a time on a computer, under the reader's control. Records were kept of the total time spent reading the passages, the time spent on each sentence and of the amount of looking back. The readers did seem to spend more time reading inconsistent paragraphs than consistent paragraphs, and they also looked back at previous information more frequently when inconsistencies were present. A full third of the inconsistencies, however, seemed to go undetected but, of course, there are several possible explanations for this. They may really have been undetected, or they may have been detected and 'fixed', or detected and ignored.

It does seem, however, that, in general, undergraduate students evaluate their own understanding during the actual process of reading. If they encounter a confusion, they give extra time to studying it and they re-read previous sentences in an effort to clarify their understanding. They also seem to be prepared to make allowances for the fact that the problem might lie in the text rather than in them. As we shall see later, this realisation is fairly late to develop in readers. The comprehension monitoring behaviour, then, of mature, skilful readers implies an active approach to gaining understanding from texts. How and when does this develop in younger and less-experienced readers?

Comprehension monitoring and listening

Although there have been a great many research studies of comprehension monitoring processes in children's reading, a significant proportion of our understandings about these processes have come from research into children's listening comprehension, a clearly parallel process. Some of this research will be outlined before we turn our attention fully to the research on reading.

The message which comes from this research is overwhelmingly that the monitoring which is needed to detect a failure in understanding is not routinely undertaken by young children. Instead, these children seem to have a tendency to think they understand what they hear when they actually do not (Brown, 1980). This phenomenon will be familiar to any teacher who has asked young children if they understand something, especially instructions. Although they will usually give a firm, positive response, their subsequent actions often belie this!

The pioneering research in this area was carried out by Markman and her associates. In one seminal study, Markman (1977) examined the extent of young children's sensitivity to their own abilities to understand instructions. Children from ages 6 to 9 were asked to help the experimenter to design a set of instructions for some new games which were to be taught to other children. The instructions suggested by the experimenter were obviously incomplete, and the test of whether a child realised that he or she had not understood was his or her request for further information. The children were given a series of prompts to jog their awareness that the instructions were unsatisfactory, the last of these prompts being a suggestion that they actually play the game. The 6-year-old children required more prompts than the older children before they indicated that they did not understand, and it also seemed that they needed to attempt to actually carry out the task before awareness dawned upon them. Markman suggests that these younger children probably failed to execute the instructions mentally and, therefore, did not notice the problems until they attempted to perform the task. The mental processing of information is clearly at the heart of the comprehension process.

Markman's findings have been echoed by those from other studies. Kotsonis and Patterson (1980) read aloud to several groups of children the rules for playing a game. The rules were read one at at time, and after each rule children were asked whether they knew how to play the game. It was found that children with normal development requested more extra rule information than learning-disabled children, and they also asked many more questions. These results were interpreted as showing that these learning-disabled children were deficient in comprehension monitoring skills.

In listening comprehension research generally, young elementary school children often say that they have understood a message even when it was incomprehensible, being either ambiguous or incomplete (Ironsmith and Whitehurst, 1978; Karabenick and Miller, 1977). They also often do not question the person providing the information, or ask for extra information when their understanding is poor (Cosgrove and Patterson, 1977). These findings are very robust, being repeated in many studies.

Young children's ascription of blame for misunderstanding of messages has also been investigated, and it appears that there might be a developmental sequence in this. Robinson (1981), in a series of experiments, investigated children's awareness that an incomplete or inconsistent message could cause a failure in communication. In a 'whose fault?' game in which the experimenter and the child took it in turns to identify a picture of an ink blot described by the other (incorrectly, in the case of the experimenter), younger children most often blamed themselves as listeners for not understanding the description. Only the oldest children began to suggest that the experimenter's descriptions were inadequate. In other studies using this 'whose fault?' game with stories about everyday life, it emerged that there was a developmental sequence from blaming themselves as listeners to blaming the quality of the information given and the speaker. When the task involved picture identification rather than stories, a similar sequence was apparent, although development seemed slower. This suggests that the nature of the task may also have some effect.

Robinson's work is significant in that it tested several important constructs, namely that:

1   the reason for a failure in comprehension may lie in the message rather than in the listener;

2   acquiring an awareness of this is a developmental process, with children progressing from blaming themselves to blaming the message and the sender;

3   the kind of task in which they have to listen can affect their awareness of their lack of understanding (Wagoner, 1983).

The picture which emerges from listening comprehension research is not always negative, however. In a study reported by Ackerman (1981), for example, a listening task was devised to try to determine if children and adults could judge if a character in a story would be able to follow realistic directions involving the time, place or nature of an everyday event. Even children of 6 years old were able to evaluate the usefulness and accuracy of most of the directions given. This is another example of the nature of the task having an effect upon children's comprehension monitoring abilities. In this case, it was suggested that the children's success was due to the realistic nature of the task they were asked to do, which was clear and purposeful and involved experiences similar to everyday life.

In other listening studies (for example, Markman and Gorin, 1981) it seemed that when children were warned in advance that the passages they were to listen to contained problems, their abilities to identify these problems improved. This may not be a terribly useful finding in practice, since in real life children are unlikely to be warned that there will be difficulties and inconsistencies in what they listen to; but it does suggest that making judgements about their actual competence in comprehension monitoring from their performance in particular contexts is fraught with difficulties.

Comprehension monitoring in children's reading

Numerous research studies have examined the operation of metacognition in children's reading, that is, their monitoring of their own comprehension. Overall, there has been a remarkable consistency in the findings of these studies and the two most replicated results have been that:

> . . . younger and poorer readers have little awareness that they must attempt to make sense of text; they focus on reading as a decoding process, rather than as a meaning-getting process.
> (Baker and Brown, 1984, p. 358)

> . . . younger children and poorer readers are unlikely to demonstrate that they notice major blocks to text understanding. They seem not to realise when they do not understand.
> (Garner and Reis, 1981, p. 571)

Looking at this research in more detail, it is apparent that there have been several distinct methodological approaches employed (these are thoroughly reviewed in Garner, 1987), some of which will be familiar from material already reviewed.

If one wishes to find out what children know, one deceptively easy way appears to be simply to ask them. Thus the interview technique has been a very popular methodology employed to try to ascertain what children thought about comprehension and reading, and whether there were any differences in their lines of thought depending on the type of reader they were. From this kind of research it has emerged that, in general, younger and poorer readers seem to have little idea that they must try to make sense of what they read; they focus instead on reading as a process of decoding the black marks on the page into sounds/words (Canney and Winograd, 1979; Myers and Paris, 1978). A fairly extensive review of research into children's concepts about reading was given in Chapter 2, and here I shall focus only on research which has explicitly enquired into children's ideas about comprehension. What does understanding involve?

What helps you to understand? What might stop you understanding? How do you know when you understand and when you do not? What are good ways of making sure you understand? What might you do if you do not understand?

These questions are listed in this way because readers might be interested to use them to frame interviews with children with whom they have contact, in order to compare their answers with the patterns which have emerged from research studies. It should be borne in mind, however, that an important drawback to this research methodology, again explored extensively in Chapter 2, is the reliability of interview data. There are many problems in asking people, and children in particular, to reflect upon their own mental processes, and there are certainly difficulties in assuming that their answers accurately reflect what these processes involve. This said, it is still true that the research findings which have emerged from this kind of enquiry are richly suggestive of important kinds of thinking in children about which teachers need to be aware.

In the study of Myers and Paris (1978), which focused upon children's metacognitive knowledge about their own reading processes, 7 to 8 year olds and 11 to 12 year olds were interviewed to try to ascertain their knowledge about themselves as readers; the activities and processes involved in reading; and the strategies appropriate to particular reading situations and purposes – in other words, their person, task and strategy knowledge. The children involved were not chosen on any ability criterion, so the results indicate simple age differences in the children's knowledge. These differences suggest that younger children lack knowledge about the reading and comprehension process. The differences can be expressed in terms of what the younger children seemed not to know which the older children did know. This included the following:

- motivation can influence the way you read and your success at it;

- different tasks demand different strategies of reading;

- one particular strategy, skimming, will enable you to focus on the most informative words in a passage;

- sentences are arranged in paragraphs in logical ways, with the first and last sentences of a paragraph being particularly important ones;

- the introductory sentence of a story usually has a special function;

- when you retell a story it is better to summarise it rather than try to retell it word for word;

- when you do not understand something, there are things you can do such as reread the text or look up a word in a dictionary.

The younger children focused quite consistently on the decoding aspects of reading, and 30 per cent of them could not think of any strategy to use when an entire sentence was not understood. Myers and Paris suggested that it might be necessary to give these readers direct instruction to alter their 'limited understanding of reading as a cognitive activity' (p. 690). (Strategies for such direct instruction and their likely effectiveness will be examined in Chapter 7.)

Forrest and Waller (1980) similarly focused their attention on the relation between children's age and their metacognitive knowledge about reading. They also extended their investigations to include the relationship between children's metacognitive knowledge and their reading achievement. They focused upon three types of metacognitive knowledge: knowledge about decoding, knowledge about comprehension, and knowledge about reading for a purpose (for example, studying). The children involved were in two age groups, 8 to 9 year olds and 11 to 12 year olds, and in each age group there were above average, average and below average readers. After individual interviews with each child, it emerged that the three variables all seemed to be affected by age and reading ability.

Moore (1983) extended the Myers and Paris study to include a comparison between children of various reading abilities and produced similar results to those of Forrest and Waller. The children in this study were of three ages, top infants (6 to 7 year olds), second year juniors (8 to 9) and top juniors (10 to 11), and in each age group high-ability and low-ability readers were included. The results suggest that the higher-ability children in each group knew more than the lower-ability children about what good readers do (person variables), the demands of particular reading tasks (task variables) and particular ways of reading in particular circumstances (strategy variables). Developments in this knowledge were apparent between the age groups, although the most noticeable growth seemed to occur between the top infant and the lower junior ages.

It seems, then, that interview-based research is fairly unanimous in suggesting that younger children (5 to 7 year olds in particular) know quite a lot less than older children (9 to 11 year olds) about themselves as readers, the reading tasks they face, and the strategies they can employ to meet the demands of these tasks (Garner, 1987). Similar differences are also apparent between children of high and low ability at reading. In particular, it seems that younger and poorer readers are less aware that they must give extra cognitive effort to making sense of the words they have decoded. They appear to lack 'sensitivity' (Flavell and Wellman, 1977) to the demands of reading for meaning (Baker and Brown, 1984).

Other research has used more direct ways of finding out what children actually do when they read and how this demonstrates comprehension monitoring. A number of studies have tried to determine the differences between good and poor readers in terms of the strategies they use as they attempt to read effectively (Golinkoff, 1975–76; Ryan, 1981).

One of the best sources of information about this kind of activity is an on-line measure obtained while a subject is actually reading, which might range from tracking eye movements to close observations of other behaviours. According to eye movement research, for example, good readers modify their eye movements when faced with difficult texts and also adapt them to fit different purposes for reading (Levin and Cohn, 1968).

Wagner and Sternberg (1987), using the term 'executive control' to describe a similar concept to what has up to now been termed 'metacognition', have attempted to isolate and measure these executive processes and assess their importance in adult reading comprehension. Their findings suggest that skilled readers monitor their ongoing reading performance and constantly revise their strategies for deriving meaning. Able readers seemed to be more likely than less-able readers to determine what they should read and how they should read it, an interesting example being their response to imminent tests about what they had read. The able readers were more likely to devote a greater amount of time to studying passages on which they knew they would have to take a detailed test, whereas less-able readers made fewer differentiations of this kind in their reading. This kind of result suggests a difference between the able and less-able readers above and beyond different decoding abilities. As Ryan, Ledger, Short and Weed (1982) note:

> Comprehension problems among unsuccessful readers with reasonably adequate decoding skills are often related to their failure to participate actively and strategically while engaged in the reading process. (p. 54)

A further way of assessing comprehension monitoring which has been used in some research studies is to ask readers to make a judgement about how certain they are that they understand a text, and then to compare their judgements with their actual comprehension as measured by a test. The hypothesis underlying this approach is that if there is a close match between judgement of understanding and actual understanding, then the readers are considered to be good comprehension monitors; and if there is a poor match, then they are poor comprehension monitors. Forrest and Waller (1979) investigated children's abilities to evaluate their own understanding using this method. Eight to nine year olds and 11 to 12 year olds, of good, average and below-average reading ability, were each asked to read two different stories. After each one, they were given a comprehension test and asked to say how confident they were that they had got the answers correct. This level of confidence was then compared to their actual scores on the test. It was found that the older and better readers were more successful at evaluating their test performance, suggesting better comprehension monitoring.

Further direct evidence of children monitoring their own understanding during reading comes from studies of self-corrections which, it is suggested, can only occur if the reader notices a problem in his or her reading. Several studies of oral reading have shown differences between good and poor readers, both in the kinds of errors they make and the incidence of spontaneous self-corrections. In the study by Clay (1972), which looked at beginning readers, the more able children spontaneously corrected 33 per cent on average of their errors, the less able only 5 per cent. Weber (1970) also found that good readers were twice as likely as poor readers to correct mistakes which did not fit grammatically in the context of the sentence. It seems from this work that good readers, even as young as 6 years old, do monitor their comprehension as they read. If they make a mistake which does not fit with the previous context, they tend to spontaneously correct it, unless the mistake still makes good sense, in which case their comprehension still appears acceptable. Beebe (1980), in a study using the miscue analysis procedure, found that children who spontaneously corrected errors as they read tended to be those who scored highest on subsequent comprehension tests. Again, the link between comprehension monitoring and comprehension itself seems quite strong, even in quite young children. Another important methodology which has produced a great many revealing research studies has involved the use of distorted texts, that is, texts containing inconsistencies of various kinds or other deliberate errors. The reasoning behind this is that readers who are actively monitoring their own comprehension will notice points at which the text fails to support their understanding. Readers who are not so 'aware' will be more likely not to notice textual problems. This methodology parallels that used in the listening comprehension research referred to earlier (cf. Markman, 1977).

Canney and Winograd (1979) used passages which were either intact or altered in ways they defined as semantic, syntactic, lexical or graphic. Able and less-able readers of 7 to 8, 9 to 10, 11 to 12 and 13 to 14 years old were asked to read these passages and to say if each was readable or not. They were then invited to explain their answers. Most of the able readers found the altered passages to be unreadable, no matter what kind of alteration they exhibited. On the other hand, the majority of the less-able readers thought most of the altered passages were quite readable. The only exception to this was the case of the passages which were graphically distorted, which all children judged to be unreadable. This suggests that a considerable amount of text disruption is required before less-able readers recognise that a problem exists within a text. Canney and Winograd link these findings to the ideas about reading which these less-able readers appeared to have, as shown in their responses to a reading concepts interview. In keeping with the bulk of research on these lines, they seemed to perceive reading as mainly about decoding rather than searching for meaning. It seems logical that if children see reading as mainly about decoding words, then they will judge text to be readable if it is composed of words they can decode. Text with distortions in its meaning will not be so much of a problem since they do not particularly expect reading to be about meaning. Yuill and Oakhill (1991) support this idea with their suggestion, based on their research into children with poor reading comprehension, that younger and poorer readers place emphasis upon trying to understand the individual words in a text rather than trying to fit together all the information contained in that text.

Winograd and Johnston (1982) asked good and poor 11- to 12-year-old readers to read short passages, each of which had an anomalous sentence near the end. They asked these children questions to try to determine whether they had detected the anomalies. As expected, the good readers were better than the poor readers at spotting the text problems, although neither of the groups managed to detect problems in all the texts. Winograd and Johnston raise the question, which was discussed earlier in relation to research studies using undergraduate student readers, of: 'Did the children fail to detect the errors or did they just fail to mention them?' (p. 69). This kind of query is important to raise because it reminds us that there is no such thing as a perfect methodology in this area, and every approach to studying comprehension monitoring brings with it problems in interpreting the results due to possible alternative explanations.

A study by August, Flavell and Clift (1984) attempts to get round this methodological problem by collecting several different kinds of data from children reading confusing passages. The children (able and less able 10- to 11-year-old readers) each read five eight-page stories. In three of these stories, a section was omitted which had the effect of making the narrative very confusing. The stories were presented to the readers one page at a time on a computer terminal. The researchers measured the time spent reading pages which followed logically from previous pages, and pages which followed illogically because of section omissions, and also noted any examples of readers going back to previous pages as they read. After the reading, they asked the readers about any errors they had found and what they had done about them. It emerged that the good readers noticed more errors, missed fewer, and used more logical strategies to cope with errors than did the poor readers. They also devoted much more time to stories which contained errors than the poor readers. Although few readers from either group looked back through texts, many of them, in both groups, showed evidence of 'fixing-up' the text to make an acceptable story from unacceptable input. Again, this is a similar strategy to that found in studies of undergraduate readers.

Other studies (Paris and Myers, 1981; Garner and Kraus, 1981–2; Garner and Taylor, 1982) have supported the main message that poorer and younger readers are less likely to notice inconsistencies in texts than better and older readers, although all readers have a tendency to make the best sense they can of texts containing problems. The Canney and Winograd (1979) suggestion that this phenomenon may be linked to children's beliefs about what they should be doing when they read, seems particularly important when seen in the light of the almost overwhelming evidence that children, probably as a result of their early reading experiences in school, tend to believe that reading is more about decoding words than searching for meaning.

Some conclusions from the research findings

While there are several questions about comprehension monitoring in reading which remain unanswered, it is possible to draw some fairly firm conclusions from the extensive research in this area. Garner (1987) sums these up well:

> The convergent findings from recent research can be summarised: young children and poor readers are not nearly as adept as older children/adults and good readers, respectively, in engaging in planful activities either to make cognitive progress or to monitor it. Younger, less proficient learners are not nearly as 'resourceful' in completing a variety of reading and studying tasks important in academic settings. (p. 59)

It appears that 'planful, strategic behaviour' (Brown, 1978, p. 457) in the face of the kind of reading tasks likely to be encountered in school learning does not develop until relatively late in children's school careers and, for some children, those who find reading difficult, this may be very late indeed. This is important because this kind of awareness is an essential ingredient in success in school.

> Part of being a good student is learning to be aware of the state of one's mind and the degree of one's understanding. The good student may be one who often says that he does not understand, simply because he keeps a constant check on his understanding. The poor student, who does not, so to speak, watch himself trying to understand, does not know most of the time whether he understands or not. Thus the problem is not to get students to ask us what they don't know; the problem is to make them aware of the difference between what they know and what they don't.
> (Holt, 1969, p. 23).

Brown (1980) argues that this is a fundamental problem for young children: being much less aware of the operations of their own minds, and much less able to introspect to find out how their minds are working, they are thus less able to exert any conscious control over their own cognition. From the research reviewed in this chapter, it seems that it is not until the middle years of schooling that children begin to be able, reliably, to show an awareness of the distinction between what they know and what they do not know, and between what they do not know at all and what they know deep down but temporarily cannot bring to mind. Brown lists some of the areas in which children's metacognitive deficiencies can cause significant problems for them in school (p. 457), and this list will serve as a summary of our present knowledge about the likely metacognitive weaknesses of young and less-able children. (This list applies to other problem-solving activities in addition to reading comprehension.) These children seem to have difficulty in:

1 recognising that the difficulty of a problem is such that they need to employ a range of strategies to deal with it;

2 using inferential reasoning to judge the likelihood that an assumption they are working with is true, given the information they already have about it;

3 predicting what will happen and what has happened as a result of their attempts to use particular strategies;

4 assessing how difficult particular tasks are in a range of problem-solving situations;

5 making forward plans for the allocation of study time on a strategic basis;

6 monitoring how successful are their attempts to learn so that they can either stop trying so hard (if successful) or try alternative strategies (if unsuccessful).

We do, therefore, have a rich research base documenting the fact of differences in the application of these strategies between various types of learners. However, as Garner (1987) points out, we lack at the moment 'a theory of the developmental mechanisms that move relatively unknowledgeable, non-monitoring, strategically naive individuals to a more metacognitively sophisticated state' (p. 31). That is, although we know that knowing and knowing about knowing and knowing how to know all get better with age and experience, we do not yet know exactly how and why this happens. This would seem an urgent question for research to focus upon in the future.

At the moment what we have are some interesting areas for speculation, which provide scope for further investigation. One of these areas centres around the fact that some studies (although by no means all; cf. the Canney and Winograd (1979) study as discussed earlier in the chapter), which have included both an interview and study of reading behaviour, have shown a lack of correspondence between what children say they would do while reading and what they, in fact, do (Garner and Kraus, 1981–2; Paris and Myers, 1981). This lack of correspondence has also been noted among undergraduate students by Phifer and Glover (1982), who descriptively entitle the report of their study, 'Don't take students' word for what they do while reading'. Medwell (1990a) has suggested that the incidence, or not, of this correspondence is problematic, largely because of the difficulty of penetrating what are, in fact, extremely complex issues by the use of a simplistic (interview) methodology. The issue needs further investigation, using more sophisticated methodologies. It is crucial, as Garner (1987) argues, to come at the problem using multiple methods: 'the better to seek converging information about "true" knowledge' (p. 82). The theoretical importance of this issue is, however, great. If a lack of correspondence between verbal knowledge and strategy use is confirmed, the direction of this incongruence will be important. It may be that readers know about a strategy some time before they actually begin to use it, that is, metacognitive knowledge precedes strategy use. Or it may be that readers begin to use a strategy unconsciously before becoming sufficiently aware of this use to be able to describe it; strategy use precedes metacognitive knowledge. Either of these sequences of learning is theoretically plausible, but each would have different implications for the possible teaching of comprehension monitoring strategies.

Another area for speculation concerns the conditions under which it seems possible to improve children's ability to spot problems and deal with them. It was earlier seen that children were more likely to be able to detect problems when they had been warned in advance to expect them (Markman and Gorin, 1981). Wagoner (1983) expresses this as, 'an induced set for problem detection apparently increases its likelihood' (p. 334), and argues that, for good and poor readers alike, being alerted in advance to the possibility of problems in a text is an effective means of making them aware of and more able to deal with these problems when they occur. The evidence for this effect is, however, very limited. Both the studies cited which show the effect have involved research on children's listening comprehension, and parallel evidence about reading has not been found. Indeed, research which has attempted to test for the effect in reading (Garner and Anderson, 1981–2) has found that alerting children to problems before their reading had little apparent effect on their detection of these problems. Garner (1987), however, puts forward a powerful argument that printed text has, for learner and fluent readers alike, an inviolability about it which produces a tendency in readers to assume that any problems they do find are more likely to be their fault than that of the text. This tendency, therefore, works against the detection of textual inconsistencies, even when the strong possibility of these has been pointed out in advance. It is clear that, in order to investigate this issue more fully, more innovative methodologies will be needed. As an example of this, the technique used by Grabe and Mann (1984) as a way of training children to detect text inconsistencies is interesting. This involved children being asked to approach texts as detectives looking for crooks who 'try to fool or mislead you' by writing 'things that sound mixed up or confused'. This is likely to make subjects much more comfortable about reporting text inconsistencies and errors and, although it was not used for this purpose in the Grabe and Mann study, does seem to have some possibilities as a way of really testing the effectiveness of alerting children to the possibility of problems in reading material.

An interesting extension to the text inviolability problem just identified concerns the idea of a possible developmental sequence which seems to be discernible through a range of listening and reading error detection studies. I earlier discussed the hypothesis of Robinson (1981) that children move from initially either not noticing textual problems or seeing them as their fault, to grasping that the problem can be in the text rather than in the person listening or reading, and then checking the text content against previous knowledge and against itself. It would be useful to explore through research the transitional points in this sequence, and any possible exceptions to it. It would also be interesting to know whether the sequence was influenced by the ways children feel, and are taught to feel by their school experiences, about themselves as readers. One might hypothesise that a classroom environment in which reading was portrayed as something you had to work hard to improve at, and in which this improvement was signalled to you by your being allowed to read harder and harder texts, might induce a feeling of assuming that all reading problems were your own fault. Conversely, a classroom environment in which you were treated as a full participant in the reading process from the very start, with a wide choice of texts and someone to read alongside you to help you tackle material you could not otherwise manage by yourself, might make you much more critical of text quality and more confident in your own ability as a reader.

The issue of classroom environment looms large in another area of speculation arising from the research on comprehension monitoring. In attempts to find explanations for the evident differences between good and poor readers in terms of comprehension monitoring, several suggestions have been made. Brown (1987) suggests that a lack of appropriate school experience might account for children's misunderstandings about reading and comprehension. There is certainly evidence to suggest that good and poor readers are treated differently in reading instruction (Au, 1980; Allington, 1983). Good readers tend to receive instruction which emphasises meaning – they are questioned about the meaning of what they read and get more opportunities to practise reading silently. They also tend to get more practice at reading in the classroom than poor readers, if only because they can do it faster. Poor readers, on the other hand, tend to receive instructions which emphasise decoding and a greater proportion of their reading experiences is performative, that is, reading aloud. Meaning is less frequently emphasised. Their school experience may, therefore, compound the problem of poor readers' over-attention to decoding at the expense of meaning.

Looking at this from a different perspective, Garner and Kraus (1981–2) suggest that school experience may actually produce metacognitive problems, and do little to alleviate them. They suggest that the way they are taught strongly influences children's perceptions of the reading process. If teaching tends to emphasise decoding and reading aloud at the expense of seeking meaning, then this is what children will try to succeed at. Good readers, so their argument proceeds, are able to go beyond this and 'experience the magic of reading for meaning' (Garner, 1987, p. 38), and change their ideas about the aims of the reading process. Poor readers, who do not encounter this 'magic' but gradually become aware of their relative status in the classroom, give even more attention to decoding in order to try to improve at reading. This 'vicious cycle' of reading perceptions and reading actions was discussed in Chapter 2.

Conclusion

This review of research into metacognition and reading has led to a position not dissimilar to that reached in previous chapters. 'Awareness' and the ability to act according to the insights it makes available are essential elements of the reading process. It is, in fact, difficult to imagine how reading could proceed in any meaningful way without this awareness. It is noticeable that currently held models of the reading process all place heavy emphasis on its planful and strategic nature, and give an important role to the 'executive'. It also seems to be the case that awareness about the purposes and strategies involved in reading is linked strongly to success in its operation, although the precise direction of this rather 'chicken and egg' relationship is not completely known. What does seem clear is that if we want children to operate metacognitively in their reading, we need to give them the opportunity and encouragement to do this, which may imply changes in the classroom ethos surrounding reading. It may also be beneficial to teach them particular strategies to enhance their comprehension monitoring. What these strategies might be, and how effective we might expect them to prove will be discussed in Chapter 7.

6 Awareness and the writing process

Introduction

> Writing allows us to think about our thinking.
> (Lucy Calkins, 1983, p. 139)

It is probably true to say that, of all the processes of literacy and language, writing is the most self-evidently metacognitive. The essence of the act of writing is the opportunity it affords us to put distance between ourselves and our thoughts. By expressing these thoughts in a visible way which we can subsequently rethink, revise and redraft, we are allowed, indeed forced, to reflect upon our own thinking. Alongside this reflection comes an enhancement in the degree to which we can be conscious – 'aware' – of these thought processes. As in the other areas of operation examined in this book, 'being aware of' one's thoughts in writing is a necessary precursor to 'being more fully in control of' the writing process. As Smith (1982) has argued, 'Writing separates our ideas from ourselves in a way that is easiest for us to examine, explore and develop' (p. 15).

The process of making thoughts external which constitutes writing has been characterised as an active dialogue between two parts of the mind: one part which might be seen as a creator of written expression and the other as a critic of this.

> The act of writing might be described as a conversation between two workmen muttering to each other at the workbench. The self speaks, the other self listens and responds. The self proposes, the other self considers. The self makes, the other self evaluates. The two selves collaborate: a problem is spotted, discussed, defined; solutions are proposed, rejected, suggested, attempted, tested, discarded, accepted.
> (Murray, 1982, p. 165)

In this dialogue approach, one side is seen as the writer and the other as the reader, but a very 'aware' kind of reader, whose roles, according to Murray, include a range of activities. This 'other self': 'tracks the activity that is taking place', 'gives the self the distance that is essential for craft', 'provides an evolving context for the writer', 'articulates the process of writing', 'is the critic who is constantly looking at the writing to see if . . . it works', 'is the supportive colleague to the writer' (Murray, 1982, pp. 166–7). It is clear that writing, seen in this way, is very much a metacognitive experience and that awareness is central to it.

> The cutting edge – the growing edge – of writing is the interactions between writers, their emerging texts and their developing meanings. The writer pulls in to write, then pulls back to ask, 'What have I said? Where is this leading me?' (Calkins, 1983, p. 138).

In this chapter, I shall examine this crucial role of metacognition in the writing process and the signs of awareness in writers. A large part of the chapter will be given to an examination of the various components of the writing process and the ways in which awareness might function at each stage. First, though, it is necessary to look more closely at what the writing process might consist of and how it is managed by accomplished and less-accomplished writers.

Models of the writing process

A number of models of the writing process have been put foward (it is normally referred to in the literature as 'the composing process' to distinguish it clearly from more limited views of writing, that is, handwriting, spelling, etc., which are themselves only components of the full process). Particularly influential models have been those of Hayes and Flower (1980) and, more recently, Bereiter and Scardamalia (1987).

Perhaps the most significant change in our understanding of the writing process has been the dramatic shift from seeing it as a linear process, in which stage follows stage, to recognising its recursive nature. Emig (1983) has contrasted views about writing arising from two kinds of thinking. On the one hand she describes 'magical thinking', which she defines as an over-simplistic linking of effect to cause as, for example, in the case of children who believe that because a cock crows at sunrise, the crowing must therefore cause the sun to rise. She parallels this with the beliefs of some teachers of writing that, because they clearly *teach* writing and their children also *learn* writing, the one must cause the other. Emig contrasts this with 'non-magical thinking' which bases itself upon the findings of research, in this case developmental research, which suggests that children learn a great deal about writing without being deliberately taught it.

(Some children, indeed, seem to learn things about writing which they are deliberately taught not to do, as in the case of 6-year-old Simon who, after several lessons, formal and informal, on how to use the full stop, was still writing lines such as: *I.lyk.tow.plaey.wiv.mi.ted*. His current theory about how full stops worked took precedence over the teaching which contradicted it.)

One of the polarities Emig suggests is between the 'common-sense' view that the writing process is essentially linear (planning takes place before transcription, transcription takes place before revision, etc.), and the research-based view that the processes of writing are recursive (revision, planning and transcription occur in varying orders and recur at various times in the writing process). Most writers will agree that in all but the simplest of writing tasks they do not move forward in a straight line from conception to completion: all planning is not completed before words are put on to paper; all the words are not on paper before writers begin to review and revise what they are writing. Writers move back and forwards among each of these components of the process. For example, as writers plan they may revise these plans even before committing anything to paper; they may formulate new plans in the very act of trying to transcribe their original ones; they may not even fully realise what the precise aims of their writing were before almost completing it (Hume, 1983).

Certainly, in terms of research into how writing is done, a linear model has proved less than useful because, as Flower and Hayes (1981) put it, it describes 'the growth of the written product, not . . . the inner process of the person producing the product' (p. 369). It is in understanding the mental processes which accompany and produce writing that a metacognitive approach is so valuable.

A recursive, non-linear model of the writing process is also useful in pedagogic terms, because it explains some of the difficulties which children might encounter as they engage in writing tasks.

Rather than thinking about static stages in the composing process, it seems more helpful to think of processes that are constantly being combined and re-combined dynamically. . . . We do plan, gather materials, search our memories, imagine our audience, make decisions about form, tone or structure, seek for the right word or image, check back over what is written, ponder about outcomes, revise and correct. However, we are rarely, if ever, doing these things one at a time. The central difficulty of writing is that it demands that we should carry out a number of these operations simultaneously.
(Protherough, 1983, p. 146)

If this model of writing as a collection of simultaneously operating and recursive processes is accurate, as suggested by an increasing volume of research (Hume, 1983), then it seems likely that great emphasis needs to be laid upon the mechanisms whereby these processes are controlled and co-ordinated in the writer. What have been termed 'executive control processes' (Raphael, Englert and Kirschner, 1989) have become a focus of interest precisely because they are a means of linking together diverse and complex component processes.

Metacognition and writing

One of the main problems in teasing out the operation of executive control processes in writing is that it all seems so obvious. Indeed, it is difficult to imagine writers with any degree of skill who are not continuously busy applying what they know about the writing process, about the structures of various text types, about purposes for writing, and about audiences, as they meld together a complex range of writing strategies and regulate their use of these strategies. However, while this is true of skilled writers, it is not so obviously true of writers who are less skilled, that is, children learning to write. It may be that one of the chief aims of instruction in writing should be to develop these executive control processes. In order to do this, it is necessary to identify areas in which instruction might be particularly valuable to learner writers as they move towards skilled, planful writing behaviour (Raphael *et al.*, 1989). The study of the metacognitive knowledge of writers will help in this.

Therefore, what does metacognitive knowledge in writing consist of? As discussed in Chapter 5, in many ways this parallels the metacognitive knowledge utilised in the process of reading comprehension. In that chapter the dimensions of personal, task and strategy knowledge were introduced as a means of classifying metacognitive knowledge about reading comprehension, and a similar classification can be used with regard to writing. I shall describe these three focal points of knowledge with reference to myself as a writer, although it is obvious, of course, that all writers are different.

Knowledge of the person

As a relatively experienced writer I know a good deal about how I write and the conditions which help and hinder this. I know, for example, that I write best, in the sense of committing words to paper, when I have a deadline which is looming, but that if that deadline becomes *too* pressing my writing performance deteriorates. I also know that in the long stretch of time between firming up an idea for writing and actually beginning to type text into the word-processor, I am engaged in what I might term 'invisible writing behaviour'. I am testing out ideas, sequences, starting and finishing points in my mind; I am reading others' writing and assimilating their ideas to my own map of the territory I want to cover, or radically changing that map to accommodate these ideas; I am talking, and arguing, about the ideas I will write about, with my wife, my colleagues, my students – in fact, anyone who might be remotely interested. I know that all these things are a normal part of writing for me and I get concerned if they do not seem to be happening for any reason. In addition, I know that when I begin to use the word-processor, however carefully I think I have worked out my map for this piece of writing, the act of writing itself will carry me off into new lines of thought and usually produce a much better end-product. I know this last fact so well that I have come to rely upon it, placing a great deal of reliance in my writing upon the inspiration of the process itself. (If for any reason this failed to work in my writing, I should be in some difficulty.)

Knowledge of the task

The majority of writing I do tends to be in a similar genre. I write mostly expository prose and, occasionally, argument. Because I do a lot of this, I know a good deal about how this kind of prose 'works': that is, I know about structuring it to make it as accessible as possible to the reader; I know about the importance of erecting 'signposts' in writing so the reader will be offered assistance through the piece (the sub-heading used at the beginning of this paragraph is an example of such a signpost); and I

know roughly who the likely audience will be for each of the pieces I
write. My knowledge about other writing tasks is not so extensive. My
experience, for example, of writing fiction, and children's fiction in particular,
has been very limited and unsuccessful, probably precisely because I have
no clear, explicit understanding of the way such text 'works'.

Knowledge of the process of writing

Being a student of writing as well as a writer (and a writer about writing),
I am in the very privileged position of knowing a fair amount about the
process of writing. The major effect of this, I am sure, is to reassure me
that the processes I go through as I write, described above, are entirely
normal and will, in the end, produce the right results. Because of this,
when I encounter a particularly trying time in my writing, I do not
panic as I once might have done, but recognise the signs of normality and
relax. (This does not always work!)

The knowledge I have just described under these three headings can enable
me to operate some executive control over writing; control which allows me
to check my own progress, choose from alternative strategies, change
direction as I proceed, and make an evaluation of the emerging and
completed product (Englert and Raphael, 1988). This personal, task
and process knowledge can, however, only operate in this way if it is
activated during the writing process. It is quite possible, as Paris (1986)
suggests, to imagine a situation in which writers might have ample
knowledge about themselves, the writing task and process, yet still fail
to implement executive control because they did not recognise the
particular situations in which they were writing as appropriate for
particular actions.

Paris, Lipson and Wixson (1983) explain this by suggesting that there are
three types of knowledge which make up the metacognitive dimension of an
activity such as writing. There is, first, a *declarative* knowledge ('knowing
that'), which includes knowledge about the structure and purposes of
particular tasks. For example, declarative knowledge includes the
knowledge that writing involves activities usually done before
transcription begins, such as a consideration of the purpose for writing
and the needs of an audience, and activities engaged in over a longer
stretch of time, such as drafting, revising and copy-editing. Secondly, there
is *procedural* knowledge ('knowing how'), which includes knowledge
about how the various actions which make up writing might be carried
out. In writing, procedural knowledge includes the writer's knowledge

that there are approaches, such as using key words or phrases to signal to potential readers about the structure of the piece of writing (internal signposts), or that writers can revise by taking out, adding in or reordering information in their pieces.

These two types of knowledge, according to Paris *et al.* (1983), fall short of constituting a strategy for writing, because they omit a strategic dimension, that is, knowledge of the circumstances in, and reasons for, which particular writing 'tactics' might be employed. This extra dimension, which they refer to as *conditional* knowledge ('knowing when and why'), addresses the exact conditions under which a writer chooses to use a particular strategy, and it is clearly a vital element in full executive control. 'An expert with full procedural knowledge could not adjust behaviour to changing task demands without conditional knowledge' (Paris, 1986, p. 119). For example, a writer may know *that* narrative is written to different rules than argumentative writing, he or she may know *how* to write in each of these genres when requested to, but he or she may still not recognise *when* either of these genres are required unless explicitly instructed. In other words, he or she has the requisite knowledge about writing, but still lacks executive, strategic control over writing.

In order, therefore, to develop children's executive control over writing, we need to make sure that children are given adequate opportunities to acquire the requisite knowledge about themselves as writers, about the writing process and about the demands of particular writing tasks, including textual structures. We must also ensure that this knowledge develops beyond simply knowing that certain things can be done in writing to knowing how they can be done and, further, to knowing when and why they should be done.

Metacognitive differences between writers

The process of establishing aims in terms of the metacognitive knowledge about writing which we would seek to develop in children is not as simple as stating the knowledge which skilled writers need. It may be that there are limitations on the extent to which primary aged children, for example, are capable of mastering and implementing this knowledge. Such limitations might be purely a function of age and maturation as writers, or they might be a product of variable skill in the process. There has been some important research in this area, particularly that of Bereiter and Scardamalia (1987), which I will examine in this section.

First, however, for a full understanding of this research, it is necessary to give some details about the methods which have typically been used to examine what are, by any token, invisible processes. This is necessary because, as with all research, methodology affects results and any critique of these results must begin with a critical appraisal of the methods used to obtain them.

The dominant method used to investigate composing processes has been protocol analysis, which has emerged as a very powerful tool for identifying and analysing psychological processes (Flower and Hayes, 1980). A protocol is an extremely detailed record of a person's writing behaviour, including observations of overt behaviour, transcribed tape recordings of the writer's verbalised thoughts while writing, as well as all the material he or she actually writes, including drafts. For a protocol, 'subjects are asked to say aloud everything they think and everything that occurs to them while performing the task' (Hayes and Flower, 1980, p. 4). In analysing these protocols, the researcher makes inferences about the psychological processes which underlie the performance of the writing task.

There are two main problems with the use of this method of gaining information about a writer's thought processes. One lies in the extent to which the verbalised thoughts ('think-alouds', as they are often termed) actually reflect the writer's real thoughts. Being asked to think aloud while performing a complex mental task is sufficiently unusual that it may be found extremely difficult by the writer, with the result that he or she articulates only a small proportion of the thoughts that actually accompany the writing. This problem is likely to be particularly acute for those writers who are forced, because of their lack of experience or the difficulty of the task in which they are engaged, to give a very high proportion of their mental attention to the writing task, that is, the younger and less-skilful writers who seem, as the discussion below indicates, to be less metacognitive about their writing than older and more skilled writers. It may be that findings which appear to demonstrate the inadequacy of younger and less-skilful writers may, therefore, be a product of the methodology used rather than of any qualitative, psychological difference.

The second problem with think-alouds is that their production may change the nature of the processes they are supposed to reflect. Writers do not normally talk to themselves while writing and it may be that, when they are asked to do this, they begin as a result to think and behave differently.

If this is the case, it is likely that they actually become *more* metacognitive about their writing, since this is what they are specifically required to do in the think-aloud.

Both these problems should be borne in mind when looking at the results of research which seems to suggest that there are differences between writers in the extent to which they are aware and in control of their own writing processes. Nevertheless, research findings in this area do seem to suggest a common pattern, namely, that older and more expert writers have greater metacognitive awareness and control over their writing than do younger and less-accomplished writers, a pattern which echoes that discussed in the previous chapter with reference to the development of reading comprehension.

Perhaps the most telling account of the differences between expert and novice writers has been that provided by Bereiter and Scardamalia (1987), drawing upon the findings of research spanning over ten years. From their own research and that of others, they affirm that studies of expert writers thinking aloud while writing provide plenty of evidence of reflective activity (Flower and Hayes, 1980, 1981). These writers continually:

- elaborate and reformulate their writing purposes and their plans for achieving these purposes;

- critically examine and revise their writing decisions;

- anticipate potential difficulties;

- make judgements and reconciliations between competing ideas;

- show an alertness to the needs of their potential and actual readership.

Such indications seem to be almost entirely absent from the think-alouds of writers of school age. Bereiter and Scardamalia show this clearly by two examples of think-alouds which accompanied the composition of a story. The first is that of an adult:

> Right now, he's isolated – and how would I . . . if I have a connection made there – how do I want to do that: do I want an adult to intervene? Or do I want this to be that realistic? Or fairy-taleish? Or . . . because I can make it any way I want. OK, maybe I . . . weird! Ah, let me see . . . I know. *He makes this model of a ship, and on this ship he makes a model of himself, and he loses it!*

The second is that of a 10-year-old child:

I could put him going to school and he probably loses a
shoe. And then he's trying to find it and someone else finds it.
And he goes home and tells his mother and his mother . . .

In both these extracts, the text in italic type actually found a representation in the text which was eventually written. This is interpreted by Bereiter and Scardamalia as showing a qualitatively different approach to composition in these two writers. The adult is more concerned with working out possibilities, that is, working on the task at an abstract level before moving on to dealing with it at a concrete level. The child, on the other hand, deals with the task only at the concrete level of 'What can I write now?'

The explanation suggested for this difference is that these writers are taking different approaches to the process of writing. Bereiter and Scardamalia claim that the procedure which novice writers follow (which they refer to as 'knowledge telling') is, in fact, a linear, non-reflective process, which consists, basically, of:

- decide what the topic is;

- tell everything you know about it.

Expert writers, on the other hand, are more likely to have or get in mind several alternative ways of handling their writing task and their writing consists of not only expressing what they wish to say, but actually working it out in the process. This 'knowledge transforming' has been described by a variety of professional writers, such as, for example, Robert Graves:

I revise the manuscript till I can't read it any longer, then I
get somebody to type it. Then I revise the typing. Then it's
retyped again. Then there's a third typing, which is the final
one. Nothing should then remain which offends the eye.
(Robert Graves in Winokur, 1988, p. 159).

It has also, according to Bereiter and Scardamalia, been found to be the process of writing used by people who do not necessarily have exceptional talents in writing, but who use writing as a means of actively reworking their thoughts. Stemming from this concept of expert writing as knowledge transforming, Bereiter and Scardamalia develop a model for the operation of reflection and awareness in the writing process.

They begin by characterising composition as a form of problem-solving, and point out the similarities between the think-alouds of writers and people engaged in more general problem-solving activities (Hayes and Flower, 1980). This problem-solving takes place in two distinct areas, and the reflective processes are seen as taking place in the resolution and links made between these two problem areas. One area, referred to as 'content space', is that in which ideas, beliefs, opinions and explanations are worked out. Questions asked in this space are of the 'What do I mean?' variety. The second area, referred to as 'rhetorical space', is that in which decisions about the expression of ideas, etc. are worked out. Questions asked in this space are of the 'What should I say?' variety. This distinction, Bereiter and Scardamalia claim, is a common one in cognitive descriptions of the process of composition.

> It is important to separate idea production from text production. The processes involved in producing text, whether they operate on the word level, the sentence level, the paragraph level, or the text level, must produce a linear sequence that satisfies certain grammatical rules. In contrast, the result of the process of idea production is a set of ideas with many internal connections, only a few of which may fit the linear model desirable for text.
> (Collins and Gentner, 1980, p. 53).

The links made between these two problem spaces may go in either direction. The content space may input into the rhetorical by questions such as, 'I have these ideas. How can I express them so that they will be best understood?'. The rhetorical may input into the content by question/ statements such as, 'That way of saying something might not be understood by everyone. Can I think of a way of elaborating on it to make it clearer? If I am going to do this I had better rethink my ideas about it so that I can be clearer myself.' Bereiter and Scardamalia contend that 'this interaction between the two problem spaces constitutes the essence of reflection in writing' (p. 302).

If this conceptualisation of the operation of reflection in writing is correct, it gives a way of accounting for the differences between novice and expert writers. Novices may be able to transfer information from content to rhetorical space, but not vice versa. This results in what Bereiter and Scardamalia term a 'think-say process of composition' (p. 304). In this process, ideas tend to be transcribed in the order in which they are generated and revisions tend to be limited to surface changes, that is, finding better ways of putting things by choosing better words or, at a lower level, correcting transcription errors. Such revisions are entirely confined to the rhetorical space. Experts compose by means of a transfer of information both from content to rhetorical space and vice versa. This results in a joint evolution of both the written composition and the writer's understanding of what he or she is trying to say.

The essence of the Bereiter and Scardamalia argument is that there are two qualitatively different models of writing, one being basically a task-execution model and the other a problem-solving model. Novice writers seem to more naturally use the former (which does not mean that they cannot under any circumstances use the latter), whereas experts have greater access to the latter. It is hypothesised that signs of a shift from knowledge-telling to knowledge-transforming would involve:

1 signs of problem-solving effort (the main feature that distinguishes knowledge-telling from knowledge-transforming being the involvement of problem-solving processes); and

2 evidence of reconsidering decisions and evaluating written products, that is, revision. The centrality of revision in any discussion of awareness in writing is dealt with later in this chapter.

Other writers and researchers have pointed to some other differences between the operation of metacognitive components in the writing of groups of writers. Englert and Raphael (1988), for example, suggest that students with learning difficulties tend to lack the metacognitive control which would enable them to implement and regulate a range of learning strategies. They seem, for example, to be less successful in regulating their textual understanding and fail to monitor or correct potential confusions as they read others' texts and produce texts themselves for others to read. This lack of ability to detect problems and to imagine the confusion which readers of their compositions may experience prevents them from successfully re-reading, monitoring and revising those texts. Such students tend to rely more on external criteria and resources (for example, teachers and/or classmates) than on their own internal resources to help them monitor the completeness and the accuracy of their texts.

Fitzgerald (1987) suggests that novice writers often lack the ability to read their own writing from the perspective of another reader. This may arise because of egocentrism which prevents these writers suppressing interpretations of their texts based on their original intentions, while taking on the viewpoint of a reader not privy to these intentions. Research findings on this point are, however, mixed. Bartlett (1982) found that elementary school children spotted more problems and revised to a much greater extent when they worked with texts which had been written by others than when working on their own texts, which suggests that egocentrism had contributed to the breakdown in their revision processes. Revision was considerably easier when the children had no personal ownership of the texts they revised. However, Bracewell, Bereiter and Scardamalia (1979) found that when children revised texts written by themselves and by others, the only difference was that they identified more spelling errors in the texts of others.

On the whole, therefore, and bearing in mind the caveat about the reliability of research methods, it does seem that younger and less-experienced writers are less able to operate metacognitively in their writing than expert writers. Indeed, it even begins to appear that it may be the level of awareness of the writing process that is itself responsible for the difference between expertise and lack of expertise in writing. This point should be borne in mind as we move to an examination of metacognitive elements in the various stages of the writing process.

The process of writing: metacognitive elements

Earlier in this chapter, mention was made of the number of attempts there have been to devise models of the writing process and a critique was presented of linear models of this. Although all formulated models of the process differ in important ways, there are also aspects which they tend to have in common. This section of the chapter will briefly examine the metacognitive dimensions of two of these aspects: those of planning what to write and of translating ideas into text. It will then go on to present a more extensive discussion of what is arguably the most significant aspect of the writing process in terms of reflection and awareness – revision.

Planning

Planning in writing occurs both before transcription begins and during transcription, and is clearly, by its very nature, a mindful activity. In order to plan the writer needs to think about, project and reflect upon what will be, might be and has been written. This demands a certain degree of distance from the actual process of putting words on to paper – a distance which is metacognitive.

The evidence from research, however, suggests that there are differences between the planning behaviours of good and not-so-good writers, differences which might be linked to the degree of awareness of their own writing processes which these writers show. It seems that good writers spend more time in planning than either average or remedial writers; they also appear to show a different balance between global planning (at the level of ideas, appropriateness, responding to audience needs, etc.) and local planning (at the level of word choice and sentence structure). Good writers tend towards the global, whereas less-skilled writers tend towards the local (Hume, 1983).

Bereiter and Scardamalia (1987) suggest that mature writers also engage in more complex planning than younger writers. From their think-alouds, it appears that the majority of what mature writers think about in terms of planning is not actually represented in their subsequent writing products. This is the opposite of findings with young writers. This suggests a greater level of awareness of the possibilities and limitations of particular writing tasks.

Thus research on planning in writing tends to support the picture of younger and less-skilled writers being less aware of their own thinking processes than mature writers.

Translating

In translating, writers must transfer ideas from their minds to visible expression in the texts they are creating. It is clear that this makes huge demands on writers' cognitive processes. Translating is an extremely complex business: writers must express ideas in written language while simultaneously dealing with problems of the coherence and structure of their texts. The list of factors to bear in mind is very extensive, for example: handwriting, spelling, punctuation, word choice, grammatical structure, cohesive ties, purpose, organisation, clarity, rhythm and the possible reactions of various possible readers. Because of this enormous range of factors, it is unlikely that any writer could maintain a state of full awareness of all of them at once. In fact, what seems to happen is that writers differ in the kinds of factors to which they do give conscious attention. Younger and less-skilled writers appear to give greater conscious attention to factors such as handwriting and spelling (Bridwell, 1981), which takes their attention *away* from 'higher order' factors. As writers become more skilful, however, so an increasing number of aspects of writing become automatic rather than requiring actively conscious attention (Hume, 1983). This means that mature writers tend to be more aware of the translating decisions they are taking, simply because they have greater capacity for attention left available to them. Again, it seems that there are differences between novice and expert writers in terms of the metacognitive aspects of their writing.

Revision

There seems little dispute that it is in the process of revision that the metacognitive dimension of writing really plays a major role. All definitions of what revision consists of assume the stepping back of the writer from what he or she has written, or is in the process of writing, in order to consider it afresh. Such a stepping back implies a necessary distancing of the writer from his or her writing, which seems the essence of metacognitive behaviour.

Several writers and researchers have attempted to define revision, and these definitions range from the ostensibly simple, such as that of Murray (1978) who defined it as 'what the writer does after a draft is completed to understand and communicate what has begun to appear on the page' (p. 87), to the more comprehensive, such as Nold's (1979) listing of its major features:

> Revising . . . is . . .
>
> 1 changing the meaning of the text in response to a realisation that the original intended meaning is somehow faulty or false or weak.
>
> 2 adding or substituting meaning to clarify the originally intended meaning or to follow more closely the intended form or genre of the text.
>
> 3 making grammatical sentences more readable by deleting, reordering and restating.
>
> 4 correcting errors of diction, transcription and syntax that nearly obscure intended meaning or that are otherwise unacceptable.
>
> (Nold, 1979, pp. 105–6)

Murray's definition is rather odd in the sense that it seems to suggest a linear model of writing (plan, then transcribe, then revise), whereas his subsequent discussion of the concept of revision makes it clear that this is not what he had in mind. Revision, he argues, is 'seeing again', which can occur at any point in the process of writing, and takes two forms: internal revision, or 'everything writers do to discover and develop what they have to say'; and external revision, or 'what writers do to communicate what they have found' (p. 91). This distinction has tended to resurface in research on the revision process and, in many ways, is similar to the concept of the two problem spaces of content (centred around the ideas of the writer) and rhetorical (centred around the demands of the reader) introduced by Bereiter and Scardamalia.

From such definitions it seems clear that revising does not simply occur after a draft is completed, but continually through the production of a piece of writing. Fitzgerald (1987) puts forward a three-part model of how revision proceeds, from a writer's identification of problems with the emerging text (perhaps arising from discrepancies between the meanings and expression of these meanings which the writer intended to produce, and those which actually seem to be emerging), to a diagnosis of these problems and how they might be ameliorated, to the final implementation of these improvements. She goes on to define revision as follows:

> Revision means making any changes at any point in the writing process. It involves identifying discrepancies between intended and instantiated text, deciding what could or should be changed in the text and how to make desired changes, and operating, that is, making the desired changes. Changes may or may not affect meaning of the text, and they may be major or minor. Also, changes may be made in the writer's mind before being instantiated in written text, at the time text is first written, and/or after text is first written.
> (Fitzgerald, 1987, p. 484)

Such a definition strongly suggests that the reviser has to be in an aware, mindful state if revision is to be possible.

As with other aspects of the writing process, there appears to be considerable variation in the amount and type of revision done by expert and less-expert (that is, lacking in skill or simply in experience) groups of writers. From early adolescence upwards, there is a tendency for the more competent writers to make many more revisions than those less competent or slightly younger, although exceptions to this have been found (Fitzgerald, 1987). Surface revisions tend to predominate, but there is also a great deal of evidence which suggests that older and/or more competent writers tend to do more revising for meaning than their younger and/or less competent counterparts. During this they make more alterations at the level of the sentence and overall theme of the writing piece (Fitzgerald, 1987). Thus a similar, developmental model of change in approaches to revision emerges to those discussed earlier with reference to other aspects of the writing process and, indeed, in the previous chapter, the process of reading comprehension. In the early stages of their development as writers, revisers concentrate on the correction of errors and the changing of surface features in their texts. As they mature, they progressively concentrate on restructuring and shaping these texts, reworking their ideas as they compose, and adjusting their writing to meet the needs of their audiences.

Young writers thus appear to find revision much harder than older writers. The reasons for this state of affairs appear not to rest in a definite lack of knowledge about how to go about making revisions. As Bereiter and Scardamalia (1987) argue, children clearly have the requisite knowledge since they can demonstrate it when forced to by particular (experimental) conditions. What they do not do is draw upon it spontaneously in circumstances when they might have been expected to do so. Bereiter and Scardamalia suggest that this is caused by the problem of attention overload, which was earlier put forward with regard to problems in translating ideas from mind into text. Faced with the heavy attention demands of revision, children adopt a strategy of 'least effort' and change what is easiest to change – which tends to be the surface aspect of writing. Only when forced to go beyond this, as in the experimental situations Bereiter and Scardamalia describe, do they draw upon the knowledge resources they have to make changes at a higher level. In normal writing circumstances, in order to make use of the relevant knowledge to make revisions beyond the surface level, children need two things, first:

> . . . to gain conscious access to these knowledge resources.
> Conscious access seems to play a larger role in revision than
> in original composition. If the only alternatives available for
> use are those that come spontaneously to mind, then

revision has little chance. The original version of the text, because it is perceptually present, has a direct claim on conscious attention. Unless the writer can deliberately bring alternatives to mind, the original text will win for lack of competition.

And secondly:

. . . an executive procedure for bringing this knowledge into use at the right times and in the proper relation to other resource demands of the task. This executive procedure must be able to switch attention from one subtask to another without disrupting progress. It must also keep the attentional burden under control without losing hold of essential elements.

(Bereiter and Scardamalia, 1987, p. 87)

Thus the key to enhancing revision among child writers seems to be assisting them to develop a greater level of conscious awareness of their own writing processes and knowledge resources. A parallel conclusion is reached by researchers who approach the question of revising strategies from an alternative perspective.

Piolat and Roussey (1991) examined the text revising strategies of adult and child writers. They based their work on the model of text revision proposed by Hayes, Flower, Schriver, Stratman and Carey (1987), which analyses the revision process into four components:

1 defining the task;

2 evaluating the text produced and defining the problems with it;

3 selecting a strategy for revision;

4 changing the text (either by modifying or rewriting it).

The first of these components is assigned a clear metacognitive role since it serves as the control manager for the rest of the process by setting the aims, constraints and criteria required to guide the revision activity. It will itself involve the operation of several types of knowledge:

- knowledge of the goals being aimed at, for example, to make the text clearer, perhaps for a specific audience;

99

- knowledge of the characteristics of the particular text (that is, its genre) and the likely influence of these structural features upon revising strategies;

- knowledge of the strategies which can be used to revise a text, for example, read it through slowly, read it through several times in succession, read sub-headings and summary passages first, etc.

Hayes *et al.* (1987) suggest that an important difference between 'expert' and 'non-expert' writers is precisely in their possession and successful application of this knowledge. Experts have much more elaborate knowledge, they are more flexible in their use of it (that is, they readily draw upon different aspects of it in response to the operation of the task), and they operate it on a wider scale (on whole texts rather than sentence by sentence).

Hayes *et al.* (1987) also analyse the choice of revising strategies open to writers and suggest that there are five:

- ignore the difficulty, either because it is judged to be trivial or too difficult to overcome;

- suspend dealing with the problem until a later time as, for example, when a writer reads through a text to check specific details and notices a different kind of problem, making a mental note to deal with it later;

- look for further information, either in the text or in memory, in order to be able to deal with the identified problem;

- re-write the text in order to preserve the idea expressed but not the means of its expression;

- revise the text to keep whatever can be saved.

Again, differences between expert and non-expert writers were found in their use of these strategies. Non-experts tended to ignore problems and rewrite more than experts, while experts tended to diagnose problems and revise more.

Piolat and Roussey (1991) examined the operation of these strategies. They proposed three hypothetical model ways in which revision strategies might be carried out, that is, three strategy sequences which would indicate a logical approach to the revision process:

- *local-to-global strategy*: writers read through their text, first to look for surface (within sentence) problems, and then to look for deeper (across sentence) problems;

- *global-to-local strategy*: writers read through their text, first to check overall appropriateness (across sentences), and then to check local problems;

- *simultaneous strategy*: writers pass through a text once only, in the correct sequence, making revisions at all linguistic levels at the same time.

They also suggested that revision might proceed in a random manner, following neither of these strategies, which would suggest a lack of conscious control of the process by the writer.

In examining the revision strategies of groups of adults and children, each group containing writers designated experts (for their age) and non-experts, they found marked differences between the strategy use of each group. Differences were also found between the revision strategies used in writing narrative texts and descriptions. To summarise these differences, it appeared that, with narratives, adults tended to use the simultaneous strategy whereas children were more likely to use the local-to-global strategy, although even this was only true of those children classed as expert writers; the non-experts did not seem to use a coherent strategy at all. The global-to-local strategy was not used at all, even by adult, expert writers. In the case of descriptions, those adults who used a coherent strategy (less than half of the sample) tended to use a local-to-global strategy, whereas a large majority of the children revised only in a random manner.

The researchers use these results to suggest that there are differences in the metaknowledge about writing which different groups of writers are able to put into the operational. The ability to bear in mind the possibility of textual problems at several linguistic levels at once (from the global, deep structure level to the local, surface structure level) seems to be the preserve of experienced adult writers only, and even they can only do this when dealing with narrative texts, in which the global structure tends to be more linearly, and familiarly, organised. Children seem not to do this even with narrative. This may be because of cognitive overload (that is, it is simply asking too much of children to expect them to operate on text at two discrete levels), or because children do not realise that they can work on their writing first for one kind of problem, then for another. Bereiter and Scardamalia's (1987) conclusion that there is a need to help children develop a greater degree of conscious awareness of their thought processes while writing, and the potential thought processes, seems particularly apt.

Implications for teaching

There are several implications which arise from the findings about awareness and the writing process which have been presented in this chapter and from other linked research. Chief among these is the proposition that teachers who wish to enable their children to develop their levels of awareness of the writing process do not simply have to wait for these children to get older and mature into more self-aware strategies. There are positive approaches which can be adopted, and research results suggest strongly that when potential problems in the operation of executive processes are minimised through supportive teacher behaviour, children tend to perform metacognitive operations, such as revision, at a much higher level than normal (Fitzgerald, 1987).

One area of such support is for teachers to make strenuous efforts to ensure that the writing experience provided for children is always meaningful and purposeful from *their* points of view. A number of studies have demonstrated positive effects from this approach as, for example, that of Robinson, Crawford and Hall (1990), who provide evidence which suggests that quite young children can develop an awareness of audience to a very marked degree when they are engaged in authentic written dialogues with other writers. Bereiter and Scardamalia (1987) provide a possible explanation for this with their concept of children's 'conditional competence' (p. 90). This involves the idea that children are capable of performing high-level mental activities in relation to writing when the task is of intrinsic worth to them, that is, when it is authentic, purposeful and self-directed. Bereiter and Scardamalia do, however, introduce a caveat to this idea with their argument that mature and successful writers are, in fact, those who are able to make tasks meaningful for themselves – this is part of the reason why they are good writers. Therefore, they claim, the teacher's provision of the 'meaningful task' is only part of the solution to the problem of ensuring development in writing. Of wider importance is the general prevalence of a knowledge-telling strategy in education, which they see as part of a general problem of a lack of attempt to promote 'intentional cognition . . . defined as the setting and deliberate pursuit of cognitive goals – goals to learn, to solve, to understand, to define and so on' (p. 361). Children's awareness of their own thought processes, in writing and other activities, would clearly be central to such intentional cognition.

Developing such awareness would appear to be possible given a reconceptualisation of the role of the teacher from direct instructor of strategies for writing to that of facilitator of children's critical appraisal of their own operation of writing strategies. This can be done as naturally as possible as part of the classroom environment by the use of such intervention procedures as questioning and conferencing, and also by ensuring that writing and revising is a sufficiently normal part of classroom life that talking about them becomes an unremarkable thing to do. Reports of the effects of such activities in primary classrooms suggest that such external support can significantly enhance children's revision activity (Calkins, 1979, 1980).

Within this naturalistic support environment, Bereiter and Scardamalia (1987) suggest a number of positive teacher strategies which focus upon the enhancement of children's awareness of the composing process. These are as follows (pp. 362–3):

1   Students need to be made aware of the full extent of the composing process. They should understand that most of it does not involve putting words on paper but consists of setting goals, formulating problems, evaluating decisions, and planning in the light of prior goals and decisions.

2   The problem-solving and planning which characterises the composing process needs to be modelled by the teacher.

3   Getting better at the composition process needs to be a clear goal in the minds of the children as well as the teacher. One way of bringing them into this is to involve them in investigations of their own strategies and knowledge.

4   Although students need a supportive and congenial environment, they also need to experience the struggles that are part of the knowledge transformation process in writing. This means pursuing challenging goals and not always writing what is most prominent in mind or what is easiest to do well.

5   Using cues and routines to help the composing process can help students acquire executive process, as long as these are given in the context of a full understanding of the process and are not simply empty tricks.

Several of these strategies will be returned to in Chapter 7, which will examine ways in which teachers might ensure an 'aware' approach to the development of literacy in the children in their care. The conclusion of the present chapter must be, as with others that have preceded it, that not only is there a place for such an aware approach to the development of literacy, but that this is an essential ingredient to effective literacy teaching.

7 Developing literacy awareness in the classroom

Introduction

At the conclusion of the previous chapter I briefly listed the implications for instructional practice put forward by Bereiter and Scardamalia (1987). Although their work was focused upon the development of composition as a whole, it is extremely interesting to note that each of their recommendations for practice are aimed at the development of children's awareness of their own thinking while composing. More explicitly than many researchers, Bereiter and Scardamalia highlight the crucial role played in the development of literacy by metacognitive as well as cognitive processes. The five areas of implications which Bereiter and Scardamalia put forward can, in fact, be used as a basis for structuring a discussion of the practical steps teachers might take to develop children's awareness in all areas of literacy. This will be done in the final section of this chapter and comparisons made with the list of guidelines which Garner (1987) puts forward for the development of an enhanced use of metacognitive strategies in teaching reading comprehension.

In the first section, I shall discuss some of the research evaluations of approaches to the direct teaching of awareness of aspects of literacy and the use of monitoring strategies. The majority of the research in this area has focused upon the development of comprehension monitoring strategies. The Bereiter and Scardamalia suggestions make it clear, however, that the principles underlying this research have application in the field of awareness of composition as well as comprehension.

Direct teaching approaches

Rowe (1988) has described the aims of instruction in metacognition as threefold:

1   To promote children's knowledge and awareness of their metacognitive activity. This might be done by, for example,

encouraging them to think aloud as they perform particular
cognitive tasks, or by getting them to keep 'think diaries' or
logs in which they record their approaches to particular
problems.

2 To facilitate a more conscious monitoring of their cognitive
activity. This might involve such activities as self-questioning
(Have I really understood this? Have I written this in the best
way?) or discussion of their work with peers and/or the
teacher.

3 To encourage them to take deliberate control over their thinking.
This might be assisted by discussing and demonstrating a
particular strategy for dealing with tasks such as reading
(an example of this is the 'Clunk-click' card suggested by
Babbs (1984) and shown in figure 7.1).

A major problem which has emerged in work on teaching this awareness
and strategy use has been that of transfer of learning. Children who
demonstrate that they have learnt to act in a particular metacognitive way
in the context of the training they have been given often seem not to
maintain this way of acting in other situations or over the longer term.
Brown, Armbruster and Baker (1986) suggest that, in order to overcome
this problem, children need to learn strategies rather than particular
techniques, strategic understanding involving a knowledge of not just
what to do but of when, where, how and why to use particular techniques.

Garner (1990) has argued that the major reason we cannot as yet
adequately explain why some metacognitive strategies do not transfer
beyond the precise context in which they were learned, and do not seem
to become established parts of learning behaviour, is that we lack a
theory of settings, that is, a theory which can explain the effects of
particular contexts upon learning and the retention and application
of learning. Particularly important in this regard is the concept which
Paris, Lipson and Wixson (1983) put forward of 'conditional knowledge',
that is, knowledge about when, why, where and how to apply particular
metacognitive strategies. Teaching should, therefore, give attention to
declarative (knowing that . . .), procedural (knowing how . . .) and
conditional knowledge.

Palincsar and Ransom (1988) outline three criteria for deciding which
monitoring strategies children should be taught. They suggest that:

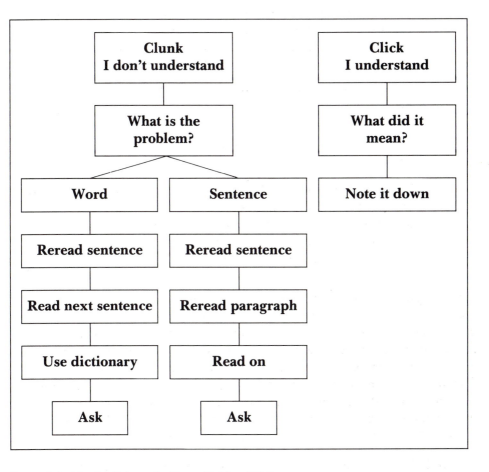

Figure 7.1 Clunk-click cards (from Babbs, 1984)

- the strategies should be capable of being used flexibly across a range of reading situations;

- the strategies should serve the twin functions of promoting the interactions of readers with texts and helping them to monitor their success at understanding the material;

- the return in terms of learning benefits provided by any strategy should justify its cost in terms of difficulty and length of teaching.

Given these criteria, there is still a great deal of evidence that teaching children metacognitive strategies can be effective. Ekwall and Ekwall

(1989) argue that differences between good and poor readers can be summarised in terms of comprehension monitoring behaviour.

Good readers:

- generate questions while they read;

- monitor and resolve comprehension problems as they read;

- are able to translate what they are reading into mental images;

- re-read when they find they have not understood a section of a reading passage.

Poor readers, on the other hand, seem to:

- lack a clear picture of the purpose of reading;

- view reading as a decoding process even though their decoding skills may be lacking;

- view reading as a passive act of translating symbol into sound;

- seldom re-read.

The aim for teachers, therefore, should be to devise ways of getting poor readers to act in the same way as good readers. Ekwall and Ekwall discuss some strategies for doing this. One, suggested by Smith and Dauer (1984), involved children reading passages and thinking about what happened to them as they read. As they suggested things such as 'I got a picture in my mind', or 'I had to read part of the passage again before I understood it', the teacher wrote down these strategies and gave each a letter code. The list of strategies with associated codes was displayed prominently in the classroom. Thereafter, the children were encouraged to note down the codes for the strategies they were using when they read. This approach, it is suggested, involved the poorer readers learning from the strategies used by the better readers. Pitts (1983), in fact, suggests that a concentration on simple strategies might be more effective than over-complication. He suggests that, in reading, children might profitably be taught to adopt such simple but effective strategies as 'ignore the difficulty and read on' and 'if the problem persists, read the section again but more slowly'.

One relatively simple procedure is that of teacher modelling. Tonjes (1988) discusses metacognitive modelling as a way of teachers demonstrating to children the monitoring strategies which they use, and Duffy, Roehler and Herrmann (1988) similarly discuss the idea of the teacher modelling mental processes to children. They argue that teachers using this approach should concentrate upon transferring metacognitive control from themselves to their children and should model mental processes – what they think as they read or write – rather than simply procedures – what they do. Only in this way, they suggest, can children learn strategies which they can apply across a range of situations rather than which are limited to the context in which they were encountered.

Another apparently beneficial strategy is that of children being taught to ask themselves questions as they read. Miller (1985) reports on a study in which 8 to 10 year olds who were explicitly taught a self-questioning procedure to accompany their reading were better able to identify inconsistencies and errors in texts (that is, according to Miller, monitor their comprehension) than other children who were directly told to look for these inconsistencies. The self-questioning procedure these children were trained to apply consisted of the following questions which they had to ask themselves as they read:

- First, I am going to decide if this story has any problems in it, like if one sentence says one thing and another sentence says something different or opposite.

- Secondly, as I read I will ask myself, 'Is there anything wrong with the story?'.

- Thirdly, I will read two sentences and stop and ask if anything is wrong.

- Fourthly, so far, so good, I am doing a great job. Now I will read the whole story and decide if there are any problems in the whole story.

- Fifthly, did I find any problems in this story?

It should be noted that this study does not provide evidence that the effects of the training would transfer to other, more self-sponsored reading tasks. It is perhaps not so surprising that children trained to alert themselves to the presence of text inconsistencies should become fairly good at spotting them. This does not necessarily mean, however, that they will have improved their abilities to monitor their own comprehension when reading texts in which there are no deliberate errors or inconsistencies.

Tregaskes and Daines (1989) report on their research into the effectiveness of the direct teaching of strategies to monitor comprehension to 12 year olds. These children were taught the following metacognitive strategies:

- *Visual imagery* (Stewart and Tei, 1984). The children were asked to visualise selected passages as the teacher read them, then to share their images by discussing and sketching them.

- *Summary sentences* (Stewart and Tei, 1984). The children were taught to omit trivial and redundant information in order to identify the main ideas of a text.

- *Webbing* (Clewell and Haidemos, 1983). The children were shown how to make concept maps of the ideas in a given passage.

- *Self-interrogation* (Brown, 1978). The children were encouraged to ask themselves questions about what they already knew about a topic and what they expected to learn from the new passage.

- *'Clunk-click' cards* (Babbs, 1984). The children were introduced to a monitoring procedure outlined for them on a personal card. A copy of this procedure is shown in figure 7.1.

Groups of children were directly instructed in these strategies over a 12-week period. After that time, they were found to perform significantly better on the testing measures than children who had not been taught the strategies. Again, however, it needs to be pointed out that these testing measures were less than satisfactory, involving, first, cloze tests in which the children received a mark only for each word they got exactly right and, secondly, error detection tests in which children had to underline words or sentences in passages which did not make sense to them. This seems a limited method of measuring improvements in comprehension and in comprehension monitoring. No attempt was made to assess whether the children's command of comprehension monitoring strategies extended to other contexts or indicated a lasting improvement.

Pramling (1988) reports on a study which, while not directly involving literacy processes, has a great deal of potential relevance to their development. Five to 7 year olds were involved in work on the theme of 'shops'. One group was taught directly about shops, largely by class question/answer sessions, and a second was encouraged to 'play' around the theme and become involved in construction, role play, etc. A third group was involved in elements of both these approaches, but was also regularly engaged in 'metacognitive dialogues' with the teacher. During these the teacher deliberately asked the children to reflect upon and discuss the ways they were going about learning and the alternative ways they might do it. As an example of this, at one point during the project, the teacher asked the children how they would set about teaching other people what they had learnt about shops. After the children had prepared several ways of approaching this (wall-charts, magazines, puppet plays, etc.) they were asked to discuss why they had chosen to present their materials in those ways. At the end of the study, all the children were asked to talk about what they thought they had learnt during the project and how they thought people learnt things. The children who had experienced the metacognitive dialogues were much more forthcoming on these questions. Pramling suggests that these children had been encouraged to be much more self-aware about their own learning.

Olson (1990) reports on a study which assessed the effects of instruction in revision strategies on the revising behaviour of 12 year olds. Some of these children were given direct instruction in revision, but were then expected to work on their writing alone; others were given no instruction, but were allowed to work on their pieces in collaboration with other children; a third group received the revision instruction *and* were allowed to collaborate in their revision. Olson found that the first group tended thereafter to make more revisions to their writing, but these were mainly of a surface nature. The quality of writing produced (in terms of rhetorical structure as well as technical accuracy) was greater in the third group, suggesting that an awareness of the need to improve the content of first draft writing and the capacity to carry this out was enhanced by direct instruction and an immediate, friendly audience on whom to test out ideas.

Haller, Child and Walberg (1988) provide a synthesis of research studies between 1975 and 1987 which have investigated the effects of training in metacognitive strategies on test scores on reading comprehension. They found overall positive effects, with the greatest effects tending to be found in those studies which involved the teaching of a variety of strategies.

From research studies such as those described, it seems that some benefical effects might arise from the direct teaching of metacognitive strategies. Approaches such as the modelling of mental processes by teachers, the encouragement of children to ask themselves questions about their own understandings and intentions and the setting of this kind of work into collaborative contexts may all be useful procedures for teachers to adopt.

Large-scale projects

Two particular projects have caused a great deal of interest in the teaching of metacognitive strategies. Each of these has shown benefits in research terms, but each has been based upon a rather different model of children's learning, an examination of which may prove interesting.

Paris, Cross and Lipson (1984) describe research into their 'Informed Strategies for Learning' programme. Starting from the beliefs that reading strategies can be explained directly to children, Paris and his colleagues put forward three principles for effective instruction:

1   children need to have the requisite declarative knowledge (knowing that), procedural knowledge (knowing how) and conditional knowledge (knowing when and why) of appropriate strategies to use in reading;

2   children can share with others their thoughts and feelings about what and how they are learning;

3   children need to be 'coached' from a position in which their learning is guided and regulated by others to a position in which they can themselves take responsibility for this.

Stemming from these principles, five techniques for teaching were developed. These were:

1   *informed teaching*: teachers explicitly told their children what a strategy involved, how it could be used and when and why they might use it;

2   *metaphors for strategies*: teachers compared particular reading strategies to other, real life, activities, for example, preparing to read a passage was compared to planning a trip;

3   *group dialogue*: teachers encouraged groups of children to discuss what they were learning from particular texts and how they were approaching the reading;

4   *guided practice*: introduction of particular strategies was followed up by specially written worksheets in which children were asked to use the strategies;

5   *bridging*: teachers periodically led lessons in which strategies they had taught were applied to other kinds of texts, drawn from a range of curriculum areas.

After a four-month programme of the teaching of 'Informed Strategies for Learning' to 8 and 10 year olds, it was found that the performance of these children on tests of comprehension monitoring (error detection tests) had increased and their awareness of reading strategies (according to their questionnaire responses) had risen. Their performance on a standardised test of reading comprehension had not, however, significantly increased (Paris and Jacobs, 1984).

Palincsar and Brown (1984) describe a training procedure which begins from a rather different model of the learning process. They argue that most training studies have produced rather discouraging outcomes, with little real impact on children's use of strategies and, particularly, on the transfer of these to activities outside those directly experienced during the training context. They attribute this failure to effect real change in learners' approaches to dealing with text to a model of learning which sees learners as simply responding, relatively passively, to instruction without really being made aware of just what they are learning and why. They claim that training, to be successful, needs to encourage learners to be active in their use of strategies and to understand why, and when, they should use the strategies to which they are introduced. The model of learning they propose as an alternative is based upon the twin ideas of 'expert scaffolding' and what they refer to as 'proleptic' teaching, that is, teaching in anticipation of competence.

This model arises from the ideas of Vygotsky (1978), who put forward the notion that children first experience a particular cognitive activity in collaboration with expert practitioners. The child is, first, a spectator as the majority of the cognitive work is done by the expert (parent or teacher), then a novice as he or she starts to take over some of the work under the close supervision of the expert. As the child grows in experience and capability of performing the task, the expert passes over greater and greater responsibility but still acts as a guide, assisting the child at problematic points. Eventually, the child assumes full responsibility for the task with the expert still present in the role of a supportive audience. Using this approach to teaching, children learn about the task at their own pace, joining in only at a level at which they are capable – or, perhaps, a little beyond this level so that the task continually provides sufficient challenge to be interesting. The approach is often referred to as an apprenticeship approach, and many teachers will be familiar with its operation in the teaching of reading (Waterland, 1985). The distance between the level at which children can manage independently and which they can manage with the aid of an expert is termed by Vygotsky as 'the zone of proximal development', and it is, according to the model, the area in which the most profitable instruction can proceed. Vygotsky claimed that, 'what children can do with the assistance of others might be in some sense even more indicative of their mental development than what they can do alone' (1978, p. 85).

Palincsar and Brown (1984) designed their comprehension monitoring teaching procedures around this apprenticeship model of learning. Their approach used what they termed 'reciprocal teaching' to focus upon four activities:

1 *summarising*: asking children to summarise sections of text, thereby encouraging them to focus upon the main ideas in a passage and to check their own understanding of these;

2 *questioning*: getting children to ask questions about what they have read, which again encourages them to attend to the principal ideas and to think about their own comprehension of these;

3 *clarifying*: asking children to clarify potentially problematic sections of text, requiring them to critically evaluate the current state of their understanding;

4 *predicting*: getting them to go beyond what the text actually says to make inferences which they have to justify by reference to what they have read.

Each of these activities had a cognitive and a metacognitive dimension in that not only were the children working upon their comprehension of the texts (comprehension fostering), but they were also having to reflect upon the extent of their comprehension (comprehension monitoring).

The reciprocal teaching procedure involved an interactive 'game' between the teacher and the learners in which each took it in turn to lead a dialogue about a particular section of text. The 'teacher' for each section first asked a question, then summarised, then clarified and predicted as appropriate. The real teacher modelled each of these activities and the role played by the children was gradually expanded as time went on from mostly pupil to mostly teacher.

This procedure was tested on a group of 11 year olds with reading difficulties. These children did initially experience some difficulties in taking over the role of teacher, and needed a lot of help in verbalising during summarising, questioning, clarifying and predicting. They did eventually, however, become much more accomplished leaders of the comprehension dialogues, and showed a very significant improvement on tests of reading comprehension, an improvement which seemed to generalise to other classroom activities and did not fade away after the completion of the research project. Palincsar and Brown attribute the success of their training programme to the reciprocal teaching procedure, suggesting that it involved extensive modelling of comprehension fostering and monitoring strategies which are usually difficult to detect in expert readers, that it forced children to take part in dialogues about their understanding even if at a non-expert level and they learnt from this engagement.

Gilroy and Moore (1988) report on the results of their replication of the Palincsar and Brown reciprocal teaching procedure with 9 to 13 year olds in New Zealand. They found that positive gains in comprehension test scores were made by these children. In a review of research on the reciprocal teaching approach, Moore (1988) agrees with the Palincsar and Brown analysis of the strengths of the approach, and suggests that it has a great deal to offer, particularly to children with identifiable weaknesses in reading comprehension.

There have, however, been criticisms of both the projects described in this section, such as that by Carver (1987) who claims that the apparent success of these training studies might be due to some other, less generalisable factors, including the increase in the time spent on teaching reading by teachers and in reading particular passages by children. The effect of the training studies described would certainly have been to cause children to spend more time in reading particular texts and this, in itself, might have accounted for their increased comprehension.

Guidelines for teaching

Using the Bereiter and Scardamalia (1987) list of implications for instruction as a basis, it is possible to put forward a number of guidelines for teaching the processes of literacy in an 'aware' way. Combining this list of implications with the guidelines for instruction suggested by Garner (1987) gives six areas for positive development. These can be expressed in terms of recommendations for teachers.

1 Understand and teach complete literacy processes and make sure children understand these processes

Bereiter and Scardamalia suggest that:

> . . . students need to be made aware of the full extent of the composing process. They should understand that most of it does not involve putting words on paper but consists of setting goals, formulating problems, evaluating decisions, and planning in the light of prior goals and decisions. (Bereiter and Scardamalia, 1987, p. 362).

Garner's first guideline supports this argument by suggesting that 'teachers must care about the processes involved in reading and studying, and must be willing to devote instructional time to them' (p. 131), and her second takes it further by recommending that teachers need to analyse in some detail just what they are asking children to do in tasks involving literacy.

The importance of this recommendation can be seen clearly when we consider the evidence such as that presented in Chapters 2 and 4 that school children tend to have very limited perceptions about the nature of reading and writing. If children see writing as largely a question of spelling correctly and transcribing neatly, and reading as a matter of decoding print to sound, they are unlikely to develop the wider awareness of literacy functions and their own mastery of these functions which is necessary for their full development. This suggests that, as a priority, teachers need to ascertain the ideas about literacy held by the children in their care, and to examine critically the messages about literacy conveyed to children by their curricula and classroom environments.

2 Model literacy processes for the children

The importance of teachers not simply telling children about the problem-solving, planning and strategic decision-making which characterises the processes of both reading and writing, but actually demonstrating these cannot be over-emphasised. Modelling enables teachers to make explicit the thought processes which accompany involvement in literate activities; processes which, by their very nature, are invisible. Unless these processes are made explicit, children can have no way of understanding what it is like to think like an accomplished reader or writer until they actually become one: in other words, much of their learning is directed towards an end of which they have no clear concept.

Modelling also functions as an important link in the chain of learning described earlier with reference to reciprocal teaching (see page 114). An apprenticeship approach is founded upon the apprentice gradually taking over responsibility for an activity, the aims and nature of which have been clearly demonstrated.

Parallels have been widely drawn between the dominant process of learning in the wider world (for example, butchers learning to be butchers, carpenters learning to be carpenters, young children learning to join in games with their older siblings) and that commonly assumed in schooling (Rogoff, 1990; Lave and Wenger, 1991). This now extensive work on the social bases of cognition suggests that learners 'participate in communities of practitioners, and that the mastery of knowledge and skill requires newcomers to move toward full participation in the sociocultural practices of a community' (Lave and Wenger, 1991, p. 29). Children are engaged in this kind of learning all the time outside of the school community, and it would seem to draw upon known strengths for school communities to become more like other communities in this regard. In literate communities, participants read and write together and several of the conditions of learning outlined by social cognition researchers can be met:

- expert readers and writers perform these activities for authentic purposes;

- accomplished and less-accomplished readers and writers engage in shared activities involving these processes;

- novices are encouraged to join in, and take over, the parts of the processes they feel they can manage ('legitimate, peripheral participation' in Lave and Wenger's terms); and

- novices are treated as if they are competent in the processes they engage in. Teachers behave 'as if the desired were actual' (Edelsky, Draper and Smith, 1983).

3 Engage the children in discussion and teaching of literacy processes

Most commentators seem to agree that an important way of enhancing children's awareness of literacy and other processes is to open up these processes to discussion by the children. By airing procedures and problems, children can be better enabled to develop fuller pictures of the processes they are working with. Bereiter and Scardamalia actually recommend the involvement of children in investigations of their own strategies and knowledge. At a simple level, this might be done by encouraging them to discuss how they went about reading or writing a particular text and how they might have done this differently.

Garner goes further in her sixth guideline by suggesting that teachers might allow children to attempt to teach each other about reading and studying processes. This might have the effect of encouraging the reflection which is essential to effective learning and, not least, of providing teachers with a window on the children's existing thought processes.

4 Make literacy challenging and involving

> Although students need a supportive and congenial environment, they also need to experience the struggles that are part of the knowledge transformation process in writing. This means pursuing challenging goals and not always writing what is most prominent in mind or what is easiest to do well.
> (Bereiter and Scardamalia, 1987, p. 363).

A similar approach could be taken to the development of reading.

It is perhaps true that, in an effort to make reading and writing accessible to children, we have sometimes oversimplified them to the extent that their challenge has been minimised and their content has been trivial. While nobody would recommend presenting literacy processes to children as difficult activities which they will find hard to master (this will only convince most children that it is not worth them trying), there still seems to be merit in making sure that children's need to be intellectually stimulated, which they all have, is satisfied in reading and writing. Certainly, most research studies into the factors influencing school effectiveness have concluded that intellectual challenge is positively linked with high achievement (cf. Mortimore, Sammons, Stoll, Lewis and Ecob, 1988).

Reading and writing can be approached as problem-solving activities in just the same way as science or mathematics, with similar enhancements in children's motivation to engage in them. This can be done through, first, the kinds of texts children are involved with. Texts such as old-fashioned reading scheme books ('Oh, oh, look Peter. Oh look Jane') offer no challenge to children in terms of ideas, but only in terms of decoding the words. It is not surprising, therefore, that children concentrate upon the one challenge to the exclusion of the other. More recently produced reading programmes, with their heavier emphasis upon quality of text, do offer more stimulating fare, and modern picture books offer a great deal of mental challenge to children as multi-layered texts (Lewis, 1990). In writing, similarly, little challenge beyond the transcription processes is offered to children by tasks such as 'Write your daily news', so they concentrate upon these aspects. Writing to sort out their ideas, in think-books or journals, for instance, concentrates upon the challenge of using writing to clarify and work out ideas – knowledge transforming.

Secondly, the social situation in which texts are written or read is important. In collaborative contexts, the quality of debate and thus thought is likely to be much higher. The benefits of such collaborative group work have been discussed at length by Bennett and Dunne (1992), and they seem to have particular applicability to the activities of literacy.

5 Teach strategies directly, but in the context of meaningful experiences

Bereiter and Scardamalia argue strongly that teaching particular cues and routines to help the composing process can help children to develop executive process, but that it can only do this if the strategies are introduced in the context of a full understanding of the process and are not simply procedural tricks. Garner supports this argument with her third guideline that 'teachers must present strategies as applicable to texts and tasks in more than one content domain' (p. 134), and her fifth, that 'teachers must provide students with opportunities to practise strategies they have been taught' (p. 136). This approach recognises that the learning of particular strategies is, first, a necessary but not sufficient part of the development of awareness about literacy and, secondly, that teaching these strategies needs to be done in such a way that children generalise them to a range of discrete contexts. To ensure that this happens, their teaching needs to be set firmly into whole, meaningful contexts rather than being presented as a series of discrete elements which children are then expected to 'bolt together' into holistic acts of literacy. This 'parts within meaningful wholes' approach has wide applicability across areas of literacy teaching. It has been argued that the teaching of the skills of reading for information is more effective if embedded within the context of children's project work (Wray, 1985), and that 'the learning . . . of skills, specific rules and conventions of English . . . are more effectively taught when based on children's own language' (D.E.S., 1978). Even in the area of phonological awareness in which the benefits of regular context-free teaching seem to have been demonstrated (Bryant and Bradley, 1985), it is possible to read an alternative interpretation. Bryant and his colleagues (Bryant, Bradley, MacLean and Crossland, 1989) have found a strong positive relationship between knowledge of nursery rhymes and phonological awareness, and it may be that a context-embedded means of developing this awareness is simply to immerse young children in rhymes.

Examples of the cues and routines which can be introduced to children to assist their self-reflection in reading and writing include cue cards such as the 'Clunk-click' cards suggested earlier, and Bereiter and Scardamalia's own suggestion of cards designed to stimulate self-questioning during writing. These contained prompts such as 'an idea I haven't considered yet is . . . ', or 'My own feelings about this are . . .'. These cues were written on pieces of card and individuals invited to 'think-aloud' about their ongoing writing. When they dried up, they chose a cue card at random and used it to continue their thinking aloud. Other routines include those listed earlier from the ideas of Tregaskes and Daines (1989).

6 Ensure that such teaching informs the whole of the literacy curriculum

Garner's fourth guideline is that instruction in metacognitive strategies should take place over an entire year, rather than in just a single lesson or unit. This idea can be taken further by saying that the development of an aware approach to literacy can never be the aim only of lessons explicitly aimed at literacy development. Literacy is used across the curriculum thus, logically, its instruction must take place across the curriculum. If some of the points made earlier, especially points 4 and 5, are accepted, then it will be seen that the most effective development of awareness of literacy is likely to take place in meaningful and challenging contexts. These are quite likely to be in areas in which children are coming to terms with content which intrigues and excites them, that is, in areas of the curriculum officially designated as science, history, geography, etc.

Conclusion

Although there are several caveats to be made about the quality of the research evidence, in particular about the measures typically used to assess children's performance during and after training experiences, it does seem that there is a good foundation for an 'aware' approach to the development of literacy. Indeed, if the arguments put forward earlier in this book are correct, it appears that there may be far more to lose by not adopting such an approach. Awareness does seem to enhance children's development of literacy, and positive teaching steps can be taken towards furthering this awareness.

The debate about the relationship between knowledge about language and competence in language use was briefly discussed in Chapter 1, and doubts expressed at that point about the direction of such a relationship. Even so, as Wallen (1994) makes clear, building a knowledge about language dimension into the primary language curriculum can have several benefits, not the least being the exciting, challenging activities it can offer children.

The relationship between literacy and awareness is, however, a good deal less problematic. There is ample evidence that there is a close relationship between skilful and appropriate use of literacy and a well-developed awareness of its purposes, its strategies and one's own competence in these. Evidence from training studies also suggests that the relationship, while clearly two way, can also act in a cause and effect manner. Of course, if children experience literacy in a wide variety of contexts, for a wide variety of purposes and through a wide variety of texts, they are likely to develop a sophisticated awareness of it. But it also seems to be the case that, by planning activities which deliberately focus upon children's awareness of literacy, teachers can help children to develop their competence in literacy.

Both of these suggestions offer real opportunities to teachers concerned with helping their pupils develop the fullest command of all the processes of literacy. Awareness and literacy go hand-in-hand and both can profitably be developed by thoughtful and imaginative teaching. What is needed is for teachers to take a 'mindful' approach to developing 'mindfulness' (Langer, 1989) in their pupils.

References

ACKERMAN, B. (1981) The understanding of young children and adults of the deictic adequacy of communications. *Journal of Experimental Child Psychology*, **31**, 256–70.

ALESSI, S., ANDERSON, T. and GOETZ, E. (1979) An investigation of lookbacks during studying. *Discourse Processes*, **2**, 197–121.

ALLINGTON, R. (1983) The reading instruction provided readers of differing reading abilities. *The Elementary School Journal*, **83**, 548–59.

ANDERSEN, E. S. (1990) *Speaking with Style*. London: Routledge.

ANDERSON, T. (1980) Study strategies and adjunct aids, in SPIRO, R., BRUCE, B. and BREWER, W. (eds.) *Theoretical Issues in Reading Comprehension*. Hillsdale, New Jersey: Lawrence Erlbaum Associates.

ASHER, S. (1980) Topic interest and children's reading comprehension, in SPIRO, R., BRUCE, B. and BREWER, W. (eds.) *Theoretical Issues in Reading Comprehension*. Hillsdale, New Jersey: Lawrence Erlbaum Associates.

ASSESSMENT OF PERFORMANCE UNIT (1988) *Language Performance in Schools*. London: H.M.S.O.

AU, K. (1980) *A test of the social organisational hypothesis: relationships between participation structures and learning to read.* Unpublished doctoral dissertation, University of Illinois.

AUGUST, D., FLAVELL, J. and CLIFT, R. (1984) Comparison of comprehension monitoring of skilled and less skilled readers. *Reading Research Quarterly*, **20**, 39–53.

BABBS, P. (1984) Monitoring cards can help improve comprehension. *The Reading Teacher*, **38**, 200–4.

BAIN, R., FITZGERALD, B. and TAYLOR, M. (eds.) (1992) *Looking into Language*. Sevenoaks: Hodder & Stoughton.

BAKER, L. (1979) Comprehension monitoring: identifying and copying with text confusions. *Journal of Reading Behaviour*, **11**, 365–74.

BAKER, L. and ANDERSON, R. (1982) Effects of inconsistent information on text processing: evidence for comprehension monitoring. *Reading Research Quarterly*, **17**, 281–94.

BAKER, L. and BROWN, A. (1984) Metacognitive skills and reading, in PEARSON, D. (ed.) *Handbook of Reading Research*. New York: Longman.

BALD, J. (1990) We learn written language much as we learn spoken language . . . against, in POTTER, F. (ed.) *Reading, Learning and Media Education*. Oxford: Blackwell.

BARTLETT, E. (1982) Learning to revise, in NYSTRAND, M. (ed.) *What Writers Know*. New York: Academic Press.

BAUER, B. and PURVES, A. (1988) A letter about success in writing in

GORMAN, T., PURVES, A. and DEGENHART, R. (eds.) *The IEA Study of Written Composition I: The International Writing Tasks and Scoring Scales*. Oxford: Pergamon.

BEEBE, M. (1980) The effect of different types of substitution miscues on reading. *Reading Research Quarterly*, **15**, 324–36.

BENNETT, N. and DUNNE, E. (1992) *Managing Classroom Groups*. Hemel Hempstead: Simon & Schuster.

BEREITER, C. and SCARDAMALIA, M. (1987) *The Psychology of Written Composition*. Hillsdale, New Jersey: Lawrence Erlbaum Associates.

BERKO, J. (1958) The child's learning of English morphology, in *Word*, vol. 14.

BOWEY, J. (1986) Syntactic awareness and verbal performance from preschool to fifth grade, in *Journal of Psycholinguistic Research*, **15**, 285–308.

BRACEWELL, R., BEREITER, C. and SCARDAMALIA, M. (1979) *A test of two myths about revision*. Paper presented at the annual conference of the American Educational Research Association, San Francisco.

BRADLEY, L. and BRYANT, P. (1983) Categorising sounds and learning to read – a causal connection. *Nature*, **301**, 419–521.

BRADLEY, L. and BRYANT, P. (1985) *Rhyme and Reason in Reading and Spelling: I.A.R.L.D. Monographs No. 1*. Ann Arbor: University of Michigan Press.

BRIDWELL, L. (1981) Rethinking composing. *English Journal*, **70**(7), 96–9.

BROWN, A. (1978) Knowing when, where and how to remember: a problem of metacognition, in GLASER, R. (ed.) *Advances in Instructional Psychology*. Hillsdale, New Jersey: Lawrence Erlbaum Associates.

BROWN, A. (1980) Metacognitive development and reading, in SPIRO, R., BRUCE, B. and BREWER, W. (eds.) *Theoretical Issues in Reading Comprehension*. Hillsdale, New Jersey: Lawrence Erlbaum Associates.

BROWN, A. (1987) Metacognition, executive control, self-regulation and other more mysterious mechanisms, in WEINERT, F., and KLUWE, R. (eds.) *Metacognition, Motivation and Understanding*. Hillsdale, New Jersey: Lawrence Erlbaum Associates.

BROWN, A., ARMBRUSTER, B. and BAKER, L. (1986) The role of metacognition in reading and studying, in ORASANU, J. (ed.) *Reading Comprehension: from Research to Practice*. Hillsdale, New Jersey: Lawrence Erlbaum Associates.

BRUCE, D. (1964) The analysis of word sounds. *British Journal of Educational Psychology*, **34**, 158–70.

BRYANT, P. and BRADLEY, L. (1983) Psychological strategies and the development of reading and writing, in MARTLEW, M. (ed.) *The Psychology of Written Language*. Chichester: Wiley.

BRYANT, P. and BRADLEY, L. (1985) *Children's Reading Problems*. Oxford: Blackwell.

BRYANT, P., BRADLEY, L., MACLEAN, M. and CROSSLAND, J. (1989) Nursery rhymes, phonological skills and reading. *Journal of Child Language*, **16**, 407–28.

CALFEE, R. (1977) Assessment of individual reading skills: basic research and practical applications, in REBER, A. and SCARBOROUGH, D. (eds.) *Towards a Psychology of Reading*. New York: Lawrence Erlbaum Associates.

CALKINS, L. (1979) Andrea learns to make writing hard. *Language Arts,* **56**, 569–76.

CALKINS, L. (1980) Notes and comments: children's rewriting strategies. *Research in the Teaching of English,* **14**, 331–41.

CALKINS, L. (1983) *Lessons from a Child.* Portsmouth, New Hampshire: Heinemann.

CANNEY, G. and WINOGRAD, P. (1979) *Schemata for Reading and Reading Comprehension Performance (Technical Report No. 120).* Urbana, Illinois: University of Illinois, Centre for the Study of Reading.

CARTER, R. (ed.) (1990) *Knowledge about Language and the Curriculum.* Sevenoaks: Hodder & Stoughton.

CARVER, R. (1987) Should reading comprehension skills be taught?, in READENCE, J. and BALDWIN, R. (eds.) *Research in Literacy: Merging Perspectives.* Rochester, New York: National Reading Conference.

CHAPMAN, J. (1983) *Reading Development and Cohesion.* London: Heinemann.

CLARK, R., FAIRCLOUGH, N., IVANIC, R. and MARTIN-JONES, M. (1990) Critical language awareness, Part 1. *Language and Education,* **4**(4), 249–60.

CLARK, R., FAIRCLOUGH, N., IVANIC, R. and MARTIN-JONES, M. (1991) Critical language awareness, Part II. *Language and Education,* **5**(1), 41–54.

CLAY, M. (1972) *Reading: the Patterning of Complex Behaviour.* London: Heinemann.

CLEWELL, S. and HAIDEMOS, J. (1983) Organisational strategies to increase comprehension. *Reading World,* **22**, 314–21.

COLLINS, A. and GENTNER, D. (1980) A framework for a cognitive theory of writing, in GREGG, L. and STEINBERG, E. (eds.) *Cognitive Processes in Writing.* Hillsdale, New Jersey: Lawrence Erlbaum Associates.

CONTENT, A., MORAIS, J., ALEGRIA, J. and BERTELSON, P. (1982) Accelerating the development of phonetic segmentation skills in kindergartners. *Cahiers de Psychologie Cognitive,* **2**, 259–69.

COSGROVE, J. and PATTERSON, C. (1977) Plans and the development of listener skills. *Developmental Psychology,* **13**, 557–64.

CRONBACH, L. (1977) *Educational Psychology.* New York: Harcourt, Brace, Jovanovich.

CRYSTAL, D. (1976) *Child Language, Learning and Linguistics.* London: Edward Arnold.

CRYSTAL, D. (1987) *The Cambridge Encyclopaedia of Language.* Cambridge: Cambridge University Press.

D.E.S. (1978) *Primary Education in England.* London: H.M.S.O.

D.E.S. (1984) *English from 5 to 16.* London: H.M.S.O.

D.E.S. (1988) *Report of the Committee of Inquiry into the Teaching of English Language.* London: H.M.S.O.

D.E.S. (1989) *English for Ages 5 to 16.* London: H.M.S.O.

D.E.S. (1990) *English in the National Curriculum.* London: H.M.S.O.

DELGADO-GAITAN, C. (1990) *Literacy for Empowerment.* Basingstoke: Falmer.

DENNY, T. and WEINTRAUB, S. (1963) Exploring first graders' concepts of reading. *The Reading Teacher,* **16**, 363–65.

DENNY, T. and WEINTRAUB, S. (1966) First graders' responses to three questions about reading. *The Elementary School Journal*, **66**, 441–6.

DONALDSON, M. (1978) *Children's Minds*. Glasgow: Fontana.

DONALDSON, M. (1989) *Sense and Sensibility: Some thoughts on the Teaching of Literacy*. Reading: University of Reading, Reading and Language Information Centre.

DONMALL, B (ed.) (1985) *Language Awareness*. London: C.I.L.T.

DOWKER, A. (1989) Rhymes and alliteration in poems elicited from young children. *Journal of Child Language*, **16**, 181–202.

DOWNING, J. (1970) Children's concepts of language in learning to read. *Educational Research*, **12**, 106–12.

DOWNING, J. (1979) *Reading and Reasoning*. Edinburgh: Chambers.

DOWNING, J. (1984) Task awareness in the development of reading skill, in DOWNING, J. and VALTIN, R. (eds.) *Language Awareness and Learning to Read*. New York: Springer-Verlag.

DOWNING, J. (1986) Cognitive clarity: a unifying and cross-cultural theory for language awareness phenomena in reading, in YADEN, D. and TEMPLETON, S. (eds.) *Metalinguistic Awareness and Beginning Literacy*. Portsmouth, New Hampshire: Heinemann.

DUFFY, G., ROEHLER, L. and HERRMANN, B. (1988) Modelling mental processes helps poor readers become strategic readers. *The Reading Teacher*, **41**(8), 762–7.

EDELSKY, C., DRAPER, K. and SMITH, K. (1983) Hooking 'em in at the start of school in a whole language classroom. *Anthropology and Education Quarterly*, **14**, 257–81.

EDWARDS, D. (1958) Reading from the child's point of view. *Elementary English*, **35**, 239–41.

EHRI, L. (1979) Linguistic insight: threshold of reading acquisition, in WALTER, T. and MACKINNON, G. (eds.) *Reading Research: Advances in Theory and Practice*. New York: Academic Press.

EHRI, L. (1991) Learning to read and spell words, in RIEBEN, L. and PERFETTI, C. (eds.) *Learning to Read: Basic Research and its Implications*. Hillsdale, New Jersey: Lawrence Erlbaum Associates.

EKWALL, E. and EKWALL, C. (1989) Using metacognitive techniques for the improvement of reading comprehension. *Journal of Reading Education*, **14**(3), 6–12.

EMIG, J. (1971) *The Composing Processes of Twelfth Graders (NCTE Research Report No. 13)*. Urbana, Illinois: National Council of Teachers of English.

EMIG, J. (1983) *The Web of Meaning*. Upper Montclair, New Jersey: Boynton/Cook.

ENGLERT, C. and RAPHAEL, T. (1988) Constructing well-formed prose: process, structure and metacognitive knowledge. *Exceptional Children*, **54**(6), 513–20.

FERREIRO, E. and TEBEROSKY, A. (1983) *Literacy before Schooling*. London: Heinemann.

FISHER, R. and SOMMERWILL, H. (1990) Writing like a reader. *English in Education*, **24**(3), 36–43.

FITTS, P. and POSNER, M. (1967) *Human Performance*. Belmont, Cal.: Brooks-Cole.

FITZGERALD, J. (1987) Research on revision in writing. *Review of Educational Research*, **57**(4), 481–506.

FLAVELL, J. and WELLMAN, H. (1977) Metamemory, in KAIL, R. and HAGEN, J. (eds.) *Perspectives on the Development of Memory and Cognition*. Hillsdale, New Jersey: Lawrence Erlbaum Associates.

FLAVELL, J. (1976) Metacognitive aspects of problem solving, in RESNICK, L. (ed.) *The Nature of Intelligence*. Hillsdale, New Jersey: Lawrence Erlbaum Associates.

FLAVELL, J. (1981) Cognitive monitoring, in DICKSON, W. (ed.) *Children's Oral Communication Skills*. New York: Academic Press.

FLOWER, L. and HAYES, J. (1980) The cognition of discovery: defining a rhetorical problem. *College Composition and Communication*, **31**, 21–32.

FLOWER, L. and HAYES, J. (1981) A cognitive process theory of writing. *College Composition and Communication*, **32**, 365–87.

FORREST, D. and WALLER, T. (1979) *Cognitive and metacognitive aspects of reading*. Paper presented at the meeting of the Society for Research in Child Development, San Fransico, March 1979.

FORREST, D. and WALLER, T. (1980) *What do children know about their reading and study skills?* Paper presented at the meeting of the American Educational Research Association, Boston, April 1980.

FOX, C. (1988) Poppies will make them grant, in MEEK, M. and MILLS, C. (eds.) *Language and Literacy in the Primary School*. Basingstoke: Falmer Press.

FOX, R. (1990) How characters become persons: the development of characterisation in children's writing, in WRAY, D. (ed.) *Emerging Partnerships: Current Research in Language and Literacy*. Clevedon: Multilingual Matters.

GARNER, R. (1987) *Metacognition and Reading Comprehension*. Norwood, New Jersey: Ablex.

GARNER, R. (1990) When children and adults do not use learning strategies: towards a theory of settings. *Review of Educational Research*, **60**(4), 517–29.

GARNER, R. and ANDERSON, J. (1981–2) Monitoring of understanding research: inquiry directions, methodological dilemmas. *Journal of Experimental Education*, **50**, 70–6.

GARNER, R. and KRAUS, C. (1981–2) Good and poor comprehender differences in knowing and regulating reading behaviours. *Educational Research Quarterly*, **6**, 5–12.

GARNER, R. and REIS, R. (1981) Monitoring and resolving comprehension obstacles: an investigation of spontaneous text lookbacks among upper grade good and poor comprehenders. *Reading Research Quarterly*, **16**, 569–82.

GARNER, R. and TAYLOR, N. (1982) Monitoring of understanding: an investigation of attentional assistance needs at different grade and reading proficiency levels. *Reading Psychology*, **3**, 1–6.

GARVIE, E. (1990) *Story as Vehicle*. Clevedon: Multilingual Matters.

GILES, H. (1971) Our reactions to accent. *New Society*, 14 October.

GILROY, A. and MOORE, D. (1988) Reciprocal teaching of comprehension-fostering and comprehension-monitoring activities with ten primary school girls. *Educational Psychology*, **8**(1/2), 41–9.

GLASS, G. (1968) Students' misconceptions concerning their reading. *The Reading Teacher*, **12**, 765–8.

GOLINKOFF, R. (1975–6) A comparison of reading comprehension processes in good and poor comprehenders. *Reading Research Quarterly*, **11**, 623–59.

GOODMAN, K. and GOODMAN, Y. (1977) Learning to read is natural, in RESNICK, L. and WEAVER, P. (eds.) *Theory and Practice in Early Reading*. Hillsdale, New Jersey: Lawrence Erlbaum Associates.

GOODMAN, K. (1976) Behind the eye: what happens in reading, in SINGER, H. and RUDDELL, R. (eds.) *Theoretical Models and Processes of Reading*. Newark, Delaware: International Reading Association.

GOODMAN, K. (1976) What we know about reading, in ALLEN, P. and WATSON, D. (eds.) *Findings of Research in Miscue Analysis: Classroom Implications*. Washington D.C.: ERIC.

GOODMAN, Y. (1983) Beginning reading development: strategies and principles, in PARKER, R. and DAVIS, F. (eds.) *Developing Literacy: Young Children's Use of Language*. Newark, Delaware: International Reading Association.

GOODMAN, Y. (1986) Children coming to know literacy, in TEALE, W. and SULZBY, E. (eds.) *Emergent Literacy*. Norwood, New Jersey: Albex.

GOSWAMI, U. (1986) Children's use of analogy in learning to read: a developmental study. *Journal of Experimental Child Psychology*, **42**, 73–83.

GOSWAMI, U. (1990) A special link between rhyming skills and the use of orthographic analogies by beginning readers. *Journal of Child Psychology and Psychiatry*, **31**, 301–11.

GOSWAMI, U. and BRYANT, P. (1990) *Phonological Skills and Learning to Read*. Hove, U.S.: Lawrence Erlbaum Associates.

GRABE, M. and MANN, S. (1984) A technique for the assessment and training of comprehension monitoring skills. *Journal of Reading Behavior*, **16**, 131–44.

GRAVES, D. (1973) *Children's writing: research directions and hypothesis based upon an examination of the writing processes of seven year old children*. Unpublished doctoral dissertation, State University of New York at Buffalo.

HALL, N. (1987) *The Emergence of Literacy*. Sevenoaks: Hodder & Stoughton.

HALLER, E., CHILD, D. and WALBERG, H. (1988) Can comprehension be taught? *Educational Researcher*, **17**(9), 5–8.

HALLIDAY, M. and HASAN, R. (1976) *Cohesion in English*. London: Longman.

HALLIDAY, M. (1971) Foreword, in DOUGHTY, P., PEARCE, J. and THORNTON, G. *Language in Use*. London: Edward Arnold.

HARRIS, J. and WILKINSON, J. (eds.) (1990) *Guide to English Language in the National Curriculum*. Cheltenham: Stanley Thornes.

HARSTE, J., WOODWARD, V. and BURKE, C. (1984) *Language Stories and Literacy Lessons*. Portsmouth, New Hampshire: Heinemann.

HAWKINS, E. (1984) *Awareness of Language*. Cambridge: Cambridge University Press.

HAYES, J. and FLOWER, L. (1980) Identifying the organisation of writing processes, in GREGG, L. and STEINBERG, E. (eds.) *Cognitive Processes in Writing*. Hillsdale, New Jersey: Lawrence Erlbaum Associates.

HAYES, J., FLOWER, L., SCHRIVER, K., STRATMAN, J. and CAREY, L. (1987) Cognitive processes in revision, in ROSENBERG, S. (ed.) *Reading, Writing and Language Learning (Vol. 2)*. Cambridge: Cambridge University Press.

HAYNES, J. (1992) *A Sense of Words*. Sevenoaks: Hodder & Stoughton.

HEATH, S. B. (1982) What no bedtime story means: narrative skills at home and at school. *Language and Society*, **6**, 49–76.

HEATH, S. B. (1983) *Ways with Words*. Cambridge: Cambridge University Press.

HOGAN, T. (1980) Students' interests in writing activities. *Research in the Teaching of English*, **14**(2), 119–26.

HOLT, J. (1969) *How Children Fail*. Harmondsworth: Penguin.

HUDSON, M. (1985) A project on spoken language for 8–10 year olds, in OPEN UNIVERSITY (ed.) *Every Child's Language: Case Studies*. Clevedon: Multilingual Matters.

HUME, A. (1983) Research on the composing process. *Review of Educational Research*, **53**(2), 210–16.

HYMES, D. (1972) On communicative competence, in PRIDE, J. and HOLMES, J. (eds.) *Sociolinguistics*. Harmondsworth: Penguin.

HYNDS, J. (1990) We learn written language much as we learn spoken language . . . for, in POTTER, F. (ed.) *Reading, Learning and Media Education*. Oxford: Blackwell.

IRONSMITH, M. and WHITEHURST, G. (1978) The development of listener abilities in communication: how children deal with ambiguous information. *Child Development*, **49**, 348–52.

IVANIC, R. (1990) Critical language awareness in action, in CARTER, R. (ed.) *Knowledge about Language and the Curriculum*. Sevenoaks: Hodder & Stoughton.

JAMES, C. and GARRETT, P. (eds.) (1991) *Language Awareness in the Classroom*. Harlow: Longman.

JOHNS, J. (1970) Reading: a view from the child. *The Reading Teacher*, **23**, 647–8.

JOHNS, J. (1974) Concepts of reading among good and poor readers. *Education*, **95**, 58–60.

JOHNS, J. (1986) Students' perceptions of reading: thirty years of enquiry, in YADEN, D. and TEMPLETON, S. (eds.) *Metalinguistic Awareness and Beginning Literacy*. Portsmouth, New Hampshire: Heinemann.

JOHNS, J. and ELLIS, D. (1976) Reading: children tell it like it is. *Reading World*, **16**, 115–28.

JOHNS, J. and JOHNS, A. (1971) How do children in the elementary school view the reading process? *The Michigan Reading Journal*, **5**, 44–53.

KARABENICK, J. and MILLER, S. (1977) The effects of age, sex and listener feedback on grade school children's referential communication. *Child Development*, **48**, 678–83.

KIRTLEY, C., BRYANT, P., MACLEAN, M. and BRADLEY, L. (1989) Rhyme, rime and the onset of reading. *Journal of Experimental Child Psychology*, **48**, 224–45.

KOLERS, P. (1973) Three stages of reading, in SMITH, F. (ed.) *Psycholinguistics and Reading*. New York: Holt, Rinehart and Winston.

KOTSONIS, M. and PATTERSON, C. (1980) Comprehension monitoring skills in learning disabled children. *Developmental Psychology*, **16**, 541–2.

KROLL, B. and ANSON, C. (1984) Analysing structure in children's fictional narratives, in COWIE, H. (ed.) *The Development of Children's Imaginative Writing.* London: Croom Helm.

LANGER, E. (1989) *Mindfulness.* Reading, Massachusetts: Addison Wesley.

LAVE, J. and WENGER, E. (1991) *Situated Learning: Legitimate Peripheral Participation.* Cambridge: Cambridge University Press.

LEWIS, D. (1990) The constructedness of texts: picture books and the metafictive. *Signal*, **62**, 131–46.

LEVIN, H. and COHN, J. (1968) Studies of oral reading: XII. Effects of instructions on the eye-voice span, in LEVIN, H., GIBSON, E. and GIBSON, J. (eds.) *The Analysis of Reading Skill.* Cornell University and US Office of Education.

LIBERMAN, I., SHANKWEILER, D., FISCHER, F. and CARTER, B. (1974) Explicit syllable and phoneme segmentation in the young child. *Journal of Experimental Child Psychology*, **18**, 201–12.

MANDLER, J. and JOHNSON, N. (1977) Rememberance of things parsed: story structure and recall *Cognitive Psychology*, **9**, 111–51.

MANN, V. (1986) Phonological awareness: the role of reading experience. *Cognition*, **24**, 65–92.

MARKMAN, E. and GORIN, L. (1981) Children's ability to adjust their standards for evaluating comprehension. *Journal of Educational Psychology*, **73**, 320–5.

MARKMAN, E. (1977) Realising that you don't understand: a preliminary investigation. *Child Development*, **48**, 986–92.

MARTIN, T., WATER, M. and BLOOM, W. (1989) *Managing Writing.* London: Mary Glasgow.

MASON, G. (1967) Preschoolers' concepts of reading. *The Reading Teacher*, **21**, 130–2.

MATTINGLY, I. (1972) Reading, the linguistic process, and linguistic awareness, in KAVANAGH, J. and MATTINGLY, I. (eds.) *Language by Ear and by Eye.* Cambridge, Massachusetts: MIT Press.

MCCONKIE, G. (1959) *The perceptions of a selected group of kindergarten children concerning reading.* Unpublished doctoral dissertation, Teachers' College, Columbia University.

MCDONALD, F. (1965) *Educational Psychology.* Belmont, Calif.: Wadsworth.

MCNAUGHTON, S. (1987) *Being Skilled: The Socialisations of Learning to Read.* London: Methuen.

MEDWELL, J. (1990a) *An investigation of the relationship between perceptions of the reading process and reading strategies of eight year old children.* Unpublished M.Ed. Dissertation, University of Wales.

MEDWELL, J. (1990b) *A study of writing contexts.* Paper presented at the 1990 World Congress on Reading, Stockholm.

MEEK, M. (1988) *How Texts Teach what Readers Learn.* Stroud: Signal Press.

MILLER, G. (1985) The effects of general and specific self-instruction training on children's comprehension monitoring performances during reading. *Reading Research Quarterly*, **20**(5), 616–28.

MOORE, P. (1983) Aspects of metacognitive knowledge about reading. *Journal of Research in Reading*, **6**(2), 87–102.

MOORE, P. (1988) Reciprocal teaching and reading comprehension: a review. *Journal of Research in Reading*, **11**(1), 3–14.

MORAIS, J., CARY, L., ALEGRIA, J. and BERTELSON, P. (1979) Does awareness of speech as a sequence of phones arise spontaneously? *Cognition*, **7**, 323–31.

MORTIMORE, P., SAMMONS, P., STOLL, L., LEWIS, D. and ECOB, R. (1988) *School Matters*. Wells: Open Books.

MURRAY, D. (1978) Internal revision: a process of discovery, in COOPER, C. and ODELL, L. (eds.) *Research on Composing: Points of Departure*. Urbana, Illinois: National Council of Teachers of English.

MURRAY, D. (1982) *Learning by Teaching*. Portsmouth, New Hampshire: Heinemann.

MYERS, M. and PARIS, S. (1978) Children's metacognitive knowledge about reading. *Journal of Educational Psychology*, **70**, 680–90.

NAREMORE, R. and HOPPER, R. (1990) *Children Learning Language*. New York: Harper & Row.

NATIONAL ASSESSMENT OF EDUCATIONAL PROGRESS (1980) *Writing Achievement 1969–79: Results from the third national writing assessment, Vol. III: 9 year olds*. Denver, Colorado: National Assessment of Educational Progress.

NATIONAL CURRICULUM COUNCIL (1992) *National Curriculum English: The Case for Revising the Order*. York: N.C.C.

NATIONAL WRITING PROJECT (1990) *Perceptions of Writing*. Edinburgh: Nelson.

NEWMAN, J. (1984) *The Craft of Children's Writing*. Ontario: Scholastic.

NINIO, A. and BRUNER, J. (1978) The achievement and antecedents of labelling. *Journal of Child Language*, **5**, 1–16.

NOLD, E. (1979) Alternatives to mad-hatterism, in MCQUADE, D. (ed.) *Linguistics, Stylistics and the Teaching of Composition*. Akron, Ohio: University of Akron.

OLSON, V. (1990) The revising processes of sixth grade writers with and without peer feedback. *Journal of Educational Research*, **84**(1), 23–9.

PALINCSAR, A. and BROWN, A. (1984) Reciprocal teaching of comprehension-fostering and comprehension-monitoring activities. *Cognition and Instruction*, **1**(2), 117–75.

PALINCSAR, A. and RANSOM, K. (1988) From the mystery spot to the thoughtful spot: the instruction of metacognitive strategies. *The Reading Teacher*, **41**(8), 784–9.

PARIS, S. (1986) Teaching children to guide their reading and learning, in RAPHAEL, T. (ed.) *The Contexts of School-based Literacy*. New York: Random House.

PARIS, S. and JACOBS, J. (1984) The benefits of informed instruction for children's reading awareness and comprehension skills. *Child Development*, **55**, 2083–93.

PARIS, S., CROSS, D. and LIPSON, M. (1984) Informed strategies for learning:

a program to improve children's reading awareness and comprehension. *Journal of Educational Psychology*, **76**, 1239–52.

PARIS, S., LIPSON, M. and WIXSON, K. (1983) Becoming a strategic reader. *Contemporary Educational Psychology*, **8**, 293–316.

PARIS, S. and MYERS, M. (1981) Comprehension monitoring, memory and study strategies of good and poor readers. *Journal of Reading Behaviour*, **13**, 5–22.

PERERA, K. (1984) *Children's Writing and Reading*. Oxford: Blackwell.

PHIFER, S. and GLOVER, J. (1982) Don't take students' word for what they do while reading. *Bulletin of the Psychonomic Society*, **19**, 194–6.

PIOLAT, A. and ROUSSEY, J-Y. (1991) Narrative and descriptive text: revising strategies and procedures. *European Journal of Psychology of Education*, **6**(2), 155–63.

PITTS, M. (1983) Comprehension monitoring: definition and practice. *Journal of Reading*, **26**, 516–23.

PRAMLING, I (1988) Developing children's thinking about their own learning. *British Journal of Educational Psychology*, **58**, 266–78.

PRATT, C., TUNMER, W. and BOWEY, J. (1984) Children's capacity to correct grammatical violations in sentences. *Journal of Child Language*, **11**, 129–41.

PROTHEROUGH, R. (1983) *Encouraging Writing*. London: Methuen.

RAPHAEL, T., ENGLERT, C. and KIRSCHNER, B. (1989) Students' metacognitive knowledge about writing. *Research in the Teaching of English*, **23**(4), 343–79.

READ, C., ZHANG, Y., NIE, H. and DING, B. (1986) The ability to manipulate speech sounds depends on knowing alphabetic spelling. *Cognition*, **24**, 31–44.

REDFERN, A. (1985) A class project on language, in OPEN UNIVERSITY (ed.) *Every Child's Language: Case Studies*. Clevedon: Multilingual Matters.

REID, J. (1966) Learning to think about reading. *Educational Research*, **9**, 56–62.

REID, J. (1972) Children's comprehension of syntactic features found in extension readers, in REID, J. (ed.) *Reading: Problems and Practices*. London: Ward Lock.

ROBINS, M. (1985) Language awareness, in OPEN UNIVERSITY (ed.) *Every Child's Language: Case Studies*. Clevedon: Multilingual Matters.

ROBINSON, A., CRAWFORD, L. and HALL, N. (1990) *Some Day You Will No All About Me*. London: Mary Glasgow.

ROBINSON, E. (1981) The child's understanding of inadequate messages and communication failure: a problem of ignorance or egocentrism?, in DICKSON, W. (ed.) *Children's Oral Communication Skills*. New York: Academic Press.

ROGOFF, B. (1990) *Apprenticeship in Thinking: Cognitive Development in a Social Context*. Oxford: Oxford University Press.

ROWE, H. (1988) Metacognitive skills: promises and problems. *Australian Journal of Reading*, **11**(4), 227–37.

RUDDELL, R. (1976) Psycholinguistic implications for a systems of communication model, in SINGER, H. and RUDDELL, R. (eds.) *Theoretical Models and Processes of Reading*. Newark, Delaware: International Reading Association.

RYAN, E. (1981) Identifying and remediating failures in reading comprehension: towards an instructional approach for poor comprehenders, in MACKINNON, G. and WALLER, T. (eds.) *Reading Research: Advances in Theory and Practice.* New York: Academic Press.

RYAN, E., LEDGER, G., SHORT, E. and WEED, K. (1982) Promoting the use of active comprehension strategies by poor readers. *Topics in Learning and Learning Disabilities*, **2**, 53–60.

SCHNECKNER, P. (1976) *The concepts of reading of selected first and third grade children and the relation of these concepts to the children's intelligence and reading achievement.* Unpublished doctoral dissertation, University of North Colorado.

SHOOK, S., MARRION, L. and OLLILA, L. (1989) Primary children's concepts about writing. *Journal of Educational Research*, **82**(3), 133–8.

SMITH, F. (1971) *Understanding Reading.* New York: Holt, Rinehart & Winston.

SMITH. F. (1977) Making sense of reading and of reading instruction. *Harvard Educational Review*, **47**(3), 386–95.

SMITH, F. (1978) *Reading.* Cambridge: Cambridge University Press.

SMITH, F. (1982) *Writing and the Writer.* London: Heinemann.

SMITH, R. and DAUER, V. (1984) A comprehensive-monitoring strategy for reading content area materials. *Journal of Reading*, **28**, 144–7.

SNOW, C. and NINIO, A. (1986) The contracts of literacy: what children learn from learning to read books, in TEALE, W. and SULZBY, E. (eds.) *Emergent Literacy.* Norwood, New Jersey: Ablex.

STEWART, O. and TEI, E. (1984) Some implications of metacognition for reading instruction. *Journal of Reading*, **27**, 36–43.

STOEL-GAMMON, C. and HEDBERG, N. (1984) *A Longitudinal Study of Cohesion in the Narratives of Young Children.* Austin, Texas: Third International Congress for the Study of Child Language.

STREET, B. (1984) *Literacy in Theory and Practice.* Cambridge University Press.

SULZBY, E. and OTTO, B. (1982) Text as an object of metalinguistic knowledge: a study in literacy development. *First Language*, **3**, 181–99.

SULZBY, E. (1986) Writing and reading: signs of oral and written language organisation in the young child, in TEALE, W. and SULZBY, E. (eds.) *Emergent Literacy.* Norwood, New Jersey: Ablex.

TAMBURRINI, J., WILLIG, J. and BUTLER, C. (1984) Children's conceptions of writing, in COWIE, H. (ed.) *The Development of Children's Imaginative Writing.* London: Croom Helm.

TEALE, W. and SULZBY, E. (1986) *Emergent Literacy.* (eds.) Norwood, New Jersey: Ablex.

TEMPLE, C., NATHAN, R. and BURRIS, N. (1982) *The Beginnings of Writing.* Boston: Allyn & Bacon.

TIZARD, B., BLATCHFORD, P., BURKE, J., FARQUHAR, C. and PLEWIS, I. (1988) *Young Children at School in the Inner City.* Hove: Lawrence Erlbaum Associates.

TONJES, M. (1988) Metacognitive modelling and glossing: two powerful ways to teach self responsibility, in ANDERSON, C. (ed.) *Reading: The ABC and Beyond.* Basingstoke: Macmillan.

TOVEY, D. (1976) Children's perceptions of reading. *The Reading Teacher*, **29**, 536–40.

TREGASKES, M. and DAINES, D. (1989) Effects of metacognitive strategies on reading comprehension. *Reading Research and Instruction*, **29**(1), 52–60.

TUNMER, W. and NESDALE, A. (1985) Phonemic segmentation skill and beginning reading. *Journal of Educational Psychology*, **77**, 417–527.

VERNON, M. (1957) *Backwardness in Reading*. London: Cambridge University Press.

VERNON, M. (1971) *Reading and its Difficulties*. London: Cambridge University Press.

VYGOTSKY, L. (1962) *Thought and Language*. Cambridge, Massachusetts: MIT Press.

VYGOTSKY, L. (1978) *Mind in Society*. Cambridge, Massachusetts: Harvard University Press.

WAGNER, R. and STERNBERG, R. (1987) Executive control in reading comprehension, in BRITTON, B. and GLYNN, S. (eds.) *Executive Control Processes in Reading*. Hillsdale, New Jersey: Lawrence Erlbaum Associates.

WAGONER, S. (1983) Comprehension monitoring: what it is and what we know about it. *Reading Research Quarterly*, **18**, 328–46.

WALLACH, G. and MILLER, L. (1988) *Language Intervention and Academic Success*. Boston: College Hill Press.

WALLEN, M. (1994) What is knowledge about language?, in WRAY, D. and MEDWELL, J. (eds.) *Teaching Primary English: The State of the Art*. London: Routledge.

WATERLAND, L. (1985) *Read with Me*. Stoud: Thimble Press.

WEBER, R. (1970) First graders' use of grammatical context in reading, in LEVIN, H. and WILLIAMS, J. (eds.) *Basic Studies in Reading*. New York: Basic Books.

WELLS, G. (1987) *The Meaning Makers*. Sevenoaks: Hodder & Stoughton.

WHIMBEY, A. (1975) *Intelligence Can Be Taught*. New York: Dutton.

WILKINSON, A. (1971) *The Foundations of Language*. Oxford: Oxford University Press.

WINOGRAD, P. and JOHNSTON, P. (1982) Comprehension monitoring and the error detection paradigm. *Journal of Reading Behavior*, **14**, 61–76.

WINOKUR, J. (1988) *Writers on Writing*. London: Headline.

WINSER, B. (1988) Readers getting control of reading. *Australian Journal of Reading*, **11**(4), 257–68.

WRAY, D. (1985) *Teaching Information Skills through Project Work*. Sevenoaks: Hodder & Stoughton.

WRAY, D. (1990) *Theoretical insights into contexts for writing*. Paper presented at the 1990 World Congress on Reading, Stockholm.

WRAY, D. (1993) Student teachers' knowledge and beliefs about language, in BENNETT, N. and CARRÉ, C. (eds.) *Learning to Teach*. London: Routledge.

YUILL, N. and OAKHILL, J. (1991) *Children's Problems in Text Comprehension*. Cambridge: Cambridge University Press.

Index